CU00455399

CONTENTS

RECIPES INDEX..103

INTRODUCTION

An air fryer oven is a full-sized oven that features an air fry cooking mode integrated within the oven cavity. With this innovative technology, you can now enjoy all of the benefits of air fry no matter what kind of range you're looking for - induction, gas, or electric. By using a high-powered fan to circulate hot air around the food at a high speed, our in-range air fry feature cooks ingredients to a perfectly crisped finish.

The Benefits of an Air Frying Oven

An air frying oven uses little to no oil to create a flavorful and crunchy texture on foods and boasts all of the same benefits as a standalone air fryer - with some additional conveniences.

1. The air fry feature is integrated right into your oven, eliminating the need to store an extra appliance or take up valuable counter space.

2. An air frying oven has more capacity, saving you time and allowing you to cook more food at once so that there's always enough for the whole family.

3. A Frigidaire Air Fry Oven does more than just air fry, so one appliance works harder for you. Enjoy other features such as Even Baking with True Convection, Fast Steam Cleaning, and Smudge-Proof® Stainless Steel.

What Foods Can You Cook in an Air Frying Oven?

An air fryer oven does a delicious job at cooking most traditional deep-fried foods and these are some of our favorites:

- Sweet Potato or French fries
- Chicken wings or tenders
- Zucchini fries
- Onion rings
- Pepperoni pizza rolls
- Mac 'n' cheese
- Brussel sprouts

How do I keep my air frying oven clean?

Before using the air fry feature, place a cookie or baking sheet a rack or two under the Air Fry Tray to catch crumbs or drips. This will keep the bottom of the oven clean and free of fallen bits that can burn or cause odors later. Remember, do not place pans directly on the oven bottom to keep heat circulating correctly.

How do I clean the Air Fry Tray?

The Air Fry Tray is dishwasher safe, but for optimal cleaning, we recommend washing it by hand. It's designed to hold foods that already have some oil on them, which should keep food from sticking.

How do I limit the amount of smoke when using the Air Fry Tray?

Air fry uses really hot air to cook food fast and make it crunchy. Although air fry uses hot air to cook, remember that you are still frying your food so that it gets crispy! When some high-fat or greasy foods (like fresh wings) meet that hot air inside an oven, some smoke is normal. **If air fry is making a lot of smoke, try these tips:**

- When using the Air Fry Tray, put a baking sheet on a rack or two below the Air Fry Tray. This keeps drips and crumbs from landing on the oven bottom, where they can burn and create smoke. For additional protection, place some foil-lined parchment paper on the baking sheet. Parchment paper traps oil and keeps it from smoking.

- Use cooking oils that can stand up to high temperatures like avocado, grapeseed, and peanut oils. Cooking sprays made from these oils are available at the grocery store.

- Keep foil, parchment paper, and bakeware off the bottom of the oven. The oven bottom needs to stay clear so air can circulate.

- Don't overcrowd the food on your baking sheet or on the Air Fry Tray. If air can't circulate around each item, the cooking and crisping process may slow down and allow more grease to settle or drip.

- If your catch-tray is smoking, try placing parchment paper on it to hold grease. For extra-moist foods, you may have to use more. It's worth it!

- Some foods, like fresh wings and some vegetables, have a lot of moisture and may drip more than you expect. For items that might drip, use a pan with low sides if you're not using an Air Fry Tray.

- Air fry uses super-heated air, so if your oven bottom already has drips or crumbs on it (it happens!), those can smoke. Keep your oven bottom clean.

- If you have an oven vent, use it when cooking with air fry, like you would when using the cooktop.

Egg Muffins

Servings: 4

Cooking Time: 11 Minutes

Ingredients:

- 4 eggs
- salt and pepper
- olive oil
- 4 English muffins, split
- 1 cup shredded Colby Jack cheese
- 4 slices ham or Canadian bacon

Directions:

1. Preheat the toaster oven to 390°F.

2. Beat together eggs and add salt and pepper to taste. Spray air fryer oven baking pan lightly with oil and add eggs. Air-fry for 2 minutes, stir, and continue cooking for 4 minutes, stirring every minute, until eggs are scrambled to your preference. Remove pan from air fryer oven.

3. Place bottom halves of English muffins in air fryer oven. Take half of the shredded cheese and divide it among the muffins. Top each with a slice of ham and one-quarter of the eggs. Sprinkle remaining cheese on top of the eggs. Use a fork to press the cheese into the egg a little so it doesn't slip off before it melts.

4. Air-fry at 360°F for 1 minute. Add English muffin tops and air-fry for 4 minutes to heat through and toast the muffins.

Baked Grapefruit

Servings: 4
Cooking Time: 20 Minutes

Ingredients:
- 1 grapefruit, cut in half
- 2 tablespoons currant jelly
- 2 tablespoons ground almonds, walnuts, or pecans
- 2 tablespoons chopped raisins

Directions:
1. Preheat the toaster oven to 350° F.

2. Section the grapefruit halves with a serrated knife. Place them in an oiled or nonstick 8½ × 8½ × 2-inch square baking (cake) pan. Spread 1 tablespoon currant jelly on each half and sprinkle each with 1 tablespoon ground nuts and 1 tablespoon chopped raisins.

3. BAKE for 20 minutes, or until the grapefruit is lightly browned.

Zucchini Walnut Bread

Servings: 6
Cooking Time: 30 Minutes

Ingredients:

- ¾ cup all-purpose flour
- ½ teaspoon baking soda
- 1 teaspoon ground cinnamon
- ⅛ teaspoon salt
- 1 large egg
- ⅓ cup packed brown sugar
- ¼ cup canola oil
- 1 teaspoon vanilla extract
- ⅓ cup milk
- 1 medium zucchini, shredded (about 1⅓ cups)
- ⅓ cup chopped walnuts

Directions:

1. Preheat the toaster oven to 320°F.

2. In a medium bowl, mix together the flour, baking soda, cinnamon, and salt.

3. In a large bowl, whisk together the egg, brown sugar, oil, vanilla, and milk. Stir in the zucchini.

4. Slowly fold the dry ingredients into the wet ingredients. Stir in the chopped walnuts. Then pour the batter into two 4-inch oven-safe loaf pans.

5. Bake for 30 minutes or until a toothpick inserted into the center comes out clean. Let cool before slicing.

6. Store tightly wrapped on the counter for up to 5 days, in the refrigerator for up to 10 days, or in the freezer for 3 months.

Berry Crisp

Servings: 4
Cooking Time: 25 Minutes

Ingredients:

- 2 16-ounce packages frozen berries or 4 cups fresh berries
- 2 tablespoons lemon juice
- ½ cup rolled oats
- 1 tablespoon margarine, at room temperature
- 3 tablespoons wheat germ
- 4 ¼ cup honey
- 5 1 teaspoon vanilla extract
- Salt to taste

Directions:

1. Preheat the toaster oven to 400° F.

2. Combine the berries or fruit and lemon juice in a 1-quart-size 8½ × 8½ × 4-inch ovenproof baking dish, tossing well to mix. Set aside.

3. Combine the rolled oats, margarine, wheat germ, honey, vanilla, and salt in a small bowl and stir with a fork until the mixture is crumbly. Sprinkle evenly on top of the berries.

4. BAKE, covered, for 20 minutes, or until the berries are bubbling. Remove from the oven and uncover.

5. BROIL for 5 minutes, or until the topping is lightly browned.

Cinnamon Sugar Donut Holes

Servings: 12
Cooking Time: 6 Minutes

Ingredients:

- 1 cup all-purpose flour
- 6 tablespoons cane sugar, divided
- 1 teaspoon baking powder
- 3 teaspoons ground cinnamon, divided
- ¼ teaspoon salt
- 1 large egg
- 1 teaspoon vanilla extract
- 2 tablespoons melted butter

Directions:

1. Preheat the toaster oven to 370°F.

2. In a small bowl, combine the flour, 2 tablespoons of the sugar, the baking powder, 1 teaspoon of the cinnamon, and the salt. Mix well.

3. In a larger bowl, whisk together the egg, vanilla extract, and butter.

4. Slowly add the dry ingredients into the wet until all the ingredients are uniformly combined. Set the bowl inside the refrigerator for at least 30 minutes.

5. Before you're ready to cook, in a small bowl, mix together the remaining 4 tablespoons of sugar and 2 teaspoons of cinnamon.

6. Liberally spray the air fryer oven with olive oil mist so the donut holes don't stick to the bottom.

7. Remove the dough from the refrigerator and divide it into 12 equal donut holes. You can use a 1-ounce serving scoop if you have one.

8. Roll each donut hole in the sugar and cinnamon mixture; then place in the air fryer oven. Repeat until all the donut holes are covered in the sugar and cinnamon mixture.

9. When the oven is full, air-fry for 6 minutes. Remove the donut holes from the oven using oven-safe tongs and let cool 5 minutes. Repeat until all 12 are cooked.

Apple Incredibles

Servings: 6
Cooking Time: 25 Minutes

Ingredients:
- Muffin mixture:
- 2 cups unbleached flour
- 1 teaspoon baking powder
- ¼ cup brown sugar
- ½ teaspoon salt
- ¼ cup margarine, at room temperature
- ½ cup skim milk
- 1 egg, beaten
- 2 tablespoons finely chopped raisins
- 2 tablespoons finely chopped pecans
- 1 apple, peeled, cored, and thinly sliced

Directions:
1. Preheat the toaster oven to 400° F.

2. Combine the muffin mixture ingredients in a large bowl, stirring just to blend. Fill the pans of an oiled or nonstick 6-muffin tin with the batter. Insert the apple slices vertically into the batter, standing and pushing them all the way down to the bottom of the pan.

3. BAKE for 25 minutes, or until the apples are tender and the muffins are lightly browned.

Garlic Basil Bread

Servings: 6
Cooking Time: 18 Minutes

Ingredients:

- Mixture:
- 3 tablespoons olive oil
- 2 garlic cloves
- ¼ cup pine nuts (pignoli)
- ½ cup fresh basil leaves
- 2 plum tomatoes, chopped
- Salt to taste
- 1 French baguette, cut diagonally into 1-inch slices

Directions:

1. Preheat the toaster oven to 400° F.

2. Process the mixture ingredients in a blender or food processor until smooth.

3. Spread the mixture on both sides of each bread slice, reassemble into a loaf, and wrap in aluminum foil.

4. BAKE for 12 minutes, or until the bread is thoroughly heated. Peel back the aluminum foil to expose the top of the bread.

5. BAKE again for 5 minutes, or until the top is lightly browned.

Cinnamon Swirl Bread

Servings: 4
Cooking Time: 50 Minutes

Ingredients:

- 2 cups all-purpose flour
- 1 cup granulated sugar
- 1 teaspoon baking soda
- ½ teaspoon table salt
- 1 teaspoon cider vinegar
- 1 cup whole milk
- 1 large egg
- ¼ cup canola or vegetable oil
- FILLING
- ½ cup granulated sugar
- 1 tablespoon ground cinnamon
- GLAZE
- ¼ cup confectioners' sugar
- 2 teaspoons whole milk

Directions:

1. Preheat the toaster oven to 350 °F. Grease the bottom of a 9 x 5-inch loaf pan.

2. Combine the flour, granulated sugar, baking soda, and salt in a large bowl. Place the vinegar in a 1-cup liquid measuring cup and add the milk; stir to combine. Whisk the milk mixture, egg, and oil in a medium bowl. Stir into the flour mixture, blending until combined.

3. Make the filling: Combine the granulated sugar and cinnamon in a small bowl.

4. Pour half of the batter into the prepared pan. Sprinkle half the cinnamon-sugar mixture over the batter in the loaf pan. Top with the remaining batter and sprinkle with remaining cinnamon-sugar mixture. Using a butter knife, make deep swirls in the batter. Make sure most of the cinnamon-sugar mixture from the top is covered in batter.

5. Bake for 45 to 50 minutes, or until a wooden pick inserted into the center comes out clean. Cool on a wire rack for 10 minutes. Run a knife around the edges of the bread, then remove the bread from the pan. Cool for an additional 10 minutes.

6. Meanwhile, make the glaze: Whisk the confectioners' sugar and milk in a small bowl until smooth. Drizzle the glaze over the partially cooled loaf. Serve warm or at room temperature.

Oatmeal Piecrust

Servings: 4
Cooking Time: 20 Minutes

Ingredients:

- 2 cups quick-cooking rolled oats
- 3 tablespoons margarine
- 1 tablespoon vegetable oil
- ½ cup confectioners' sugar
- Salt to taste

Directions:

1. Preheat the toaster oven to 350° F.

2. Combine all the ingredients with a fork in a medium bowl, blending well and adding a little water if the mixture is too crumbly.

3. Press the mixture into a 9¾-inch round pie pan. The crust must be even in thickness.

4. BAKE for 20 minutes, or until the crust is lightly browned. Cool before filling.

Spinach, Tomato & Feta Quiche

Servings: 8
Cooking Time: 60 Minutes

Ingredients:

- Pie Crust Ingredients
- 1½ cups all-purpose flour, plus more for dusting
- ½ teaspoon kosher salt
- 3 tablespoons unsalted butter, chilled and cubed
- 6 tablespoons vegetable shortening, chilled
- 3 tablespoons ice water
- Dry beans or uncooked rice, for filling
- Filling Ingredients
- 1½ ounces frozen spinach, thawed and squeezed dry
- 9 cherry tomatoes, halved
- 1½ ounces crumbled feta cheese 4 large eggs
- ½ cup heavy cream
- ½ teaspoon kosher salt
- ¼ teaspoon freshly ground black pepper
- Extra virgin olive oil, for drizzling

Directions:

1. Combine the flour and salt in a food processor and pulse once to combine.

2. Add the butter and shortening, then pulse until the mixture creates fine crumbs.

3. Pour the water in slowly and pulse until it forms a dough.

4. Form the dough into a square, wrap with plastic wrap, and place in the fridge for 6 hours or overnight.

5. Remove the dough from the fridge, unwrap it, and place onto a lightly floured work surface.

6. Roll out the dough into a 10-inch diameter circle. You may need to use additional flour to keep the dough from sticking to the rolling pin.

7. Place the dough into the tart pan and use your fingers to form the dough to fit the pan.

8. Trim the edges and prick the bottom of the tart shell all over.

9. Cover with plastic wrap and place in the freezer for 30 minutes.

10. Remove from the freezer, unwrap, and top with parchment paper that covers all the edges.

11. Fill the tart shell with dry beans or uncooked rice until the dough is fully covered. Set aside.

12. Preheat the toaster Oven to 350°F.

13. Place the tart shell on the wire rack, then insert the rack at low position in the preheated oven.

14. Select the Bake function, press the Fan/Light button to start the fan, then press Start/Pause.

15. Remove the tart shell from the oven and let it cool for 1 hour.

16. Arrange the spinach, tomatoes, and feta cheese evenly inside the empty tart shell.

17. Whisk together the eggs, heavy cream, salt, and pepper until well combined.

18. Pour the egg mixture into the filled tart shell and lightly drizzle with extra-virgin olive oil. You may have some extra filling left over.

19. Preheat the toaster Oven to 350°F.

20. Place the quiche on the wire rack, then insert the rack at low position in the preheated oven.

21. Select the Bake function, then press Start/Pause.

22. Remove the quiche from the oven and let it cool for 5 minutes.

23. Cut into slices and serve.

Hot Italian-style Sub

Servings:3
Cooking Time: 15 Minutes

Ingredients:

- 3 Italian-style hoagie rolls
- 3 tablespoons unsalted butter, softened
- 1 teaspoon Italian seasoning
- ½ teaspoon garlic powder
- 9 slices salami
- 12 slices pepperoni
- 3 thin slices ham
- 3 tablespoons giardiniera mix, chopped
- 6 tablespoons shredded mozzarella cheese

Directions:

1. Preheat the toaster oven to 350°F. Split the rolls lengthwise, cutting almost but not quite though the roll. Place the sandwiches in a 12 x 12-inch baking pan, side by side with the open side face up.

2. Combine the butter, Italian seasoning, and garlic powder in a small bowl. Spread evenly on the inside of the hoagie rolls.

3. Layer a third of the salami, pepperoni, and ham on each sandwich. Sprinkle with the giardiniera mix and mozzarella cheese.

4. Bake for 10 to 15 minutes or until heated through and the cheese is melted.

Best-ever Cinnamon Rolls

Servings: 10
Cooking Time: 18 Minutes

Ingredients:

- 1 tablespoon unsalted butter, softened
- DOUGH
- ½ cup whole milk
- 2 tablespoons unsalted butter, softened
- 3 tablespoons granulated sugar
- ½ teaspoon table salt
- 1 large egg
- 1 ⅔ cups all-purpose flour, plus more for kneading and dusting
- 1 ¼ teaspoons instant yeast
- FILLING
- ⅔ cup packed dark brown sugar
- 1 tablespoon plus 1 teaspoon ground cinnamon
- Pinch table salt
- 3 tablespoons unsalted butter, melted
- GLAZE
- 1 ½ cups confectioners' sugar
- 1 to 2 tablespoon whole milk
- 1 tablespoon brewed coffee
- ½ teaspoon pure vanilla extract
- 1 tablespoon unsalted butter, melted

Directions:

1. Spread the 1 tablespoon softened butter generously on the sides and bottom of an 8-inch round baking pan.

2. Combine the milk, 2 tablespoons softened butter, sugar, and salt in a 4-cup glass measuring cup. Microwave on High (100 percent) power for 40 seconds or until warm (110°F). (All the butter may not melt.) Whisk in the egg.

3. Stir the flour and yeast in a large bowl. Add the liquid ingredients and stir until you have a soft dough. Flour your hands and a clean surface. Transfer the dough to the floured surface and form it into a ball. Add flour as necessary and knead by pressing the dough with the heel of your hands and turning and repeating. Add just enough flour to keep the dough from being sticky.

4. When the dough is smooth and springs back when you press it with you finger (after 3 to 5 minutes of kneading), place the dough ball into a large oiled bowl, cover with a tea towel, and let rise in a warm place for about an hour or until the dough has almost doubled in size.

5. Transfer the dough to a floured surface and roll into a 10 x 14-inch rectangle.

6. Make the filling: Combine the brown sugar, cinnamon, and salt in a small bowl. Using a pastry brush, brush the melted butter over the entire surface of the dough. Sprinkle the cinnamon-sugar mixture over the butter, using your fingers to lightly press the mixture into the dough. Starting with the longer side, roll up the dough to form a 14-inch cylinder. Gently cut the cylinder into 10 even rolls, using a serrated knife. Place in the prepared pan, cut side up. Cover and let rise in a warm place for about 45 to 60 minutes or until doubled.

7. Preheat the toaster oven to 350°F. Bake for 16 to 18 minutes or until slightly brown on top. Remove from the oven and place on a wire rack.

8. Meanwhile, make the glaze: Whisk the confectioners' sugar, 1 tablespoon milk, the coffee, vanilla, and butter in a medium bowl. If needed, whisk in the additional milk to make the desired consistency. Drizzle over the warm rolls.

Onion And Cheese Buttermilk Biscuits

Servings: 4

Cooking Time: 15 Minutes

Ingredients:

- 2 cups unbleached flour
- 3 tablespoons margarine, at room temperature
- ¾ cup low-fat buttermilk
- 4 teaspoons baking powder
- 1 teaspoon garlic powder
- ¼ cup grated Parmesan cheese
- 3 tablespoons finely chopped onion
- 2 tablespoons chopped fresh parsley
- Salt to taste

Directions:

1. Preheat the toaster oven to 400° F.

2. Blend all the ingredients in a medium bowl with a fork, then press together to form a dough ball.

3. KNEAD the dough on a lightly floured surface just until smooth.

4. Roll the dough to ½-inch thickness and cut with a round 3-inch cookie cutter. Place on an oiled or nonstick 6½ × 10-inch baking sheet or in an oiled or nonstick 8½ × 8½ × 2-inch square baking (cake) pan.

5. BAKE for 15 minutes, or until lightly browned.

Spicy Oven-baked Chili

Servings: 6
Cooking Time: 30 Minutes

Ingredients:

- 1 pound lean ground turkey or ground chicken breast or 1 pound lean ground sirloin or round steak
- 1 15-ounce can black beans, drained
- 1 8-ounce can tomato sauce
- ¾ cup chopped onion
- ¼ cup dry white wine
- 1 cup tomato salsa
- 1 tablespoon garlic powder
- 1 tablespoon chili powder
- 2 ⅛ teaspoon cayenne
- 3 teaspoons unsweetened cocoa
- Salt and butcher's pepper to taste

Directions:

1. Preheat the toaster oven to 375° F.

2. Combine all the ingredients in a 1-quart 8½ × 8½ × 4-inch ovenproof baking dish and mix well. Adjust the seasonings to taste. Cover with aluminum foil.

3. BAKE, covered, for 30 minutes.

Pork And Brown Rice Casserole

Servings: 4
Cooking Time: 45 Minutes

Ingredients:

- 2 very lean 6-ounce boneless pork chops, cut into 1-inch cubes
- ½ cup brown rice
- 1 cup chunky tomato sauce
- ½ cup dry white wine
- 3 tablespoons finely chopped onion
- 2 small zucchini squashes, finely chopped
- 2 plum tomatoes, chopped
- ½ teaspoon ground cumin
- ½ teaspoon ground ginger
- 1 teaspoon garlic powder
- 2 bay leaves
- Salt and freshly ground black pepper

Directions:

1. Preheat the toaster oven to 400° F.

2. Combine all the ingredients in a 1-quart 8½ × 8½ × 4-inch ovenproof baking dish. Cover with aluminum foil.

3. BAKE, covered, for 45 minutes, or until the rice is cooked to your preference. Discard the bay leaves before serving.

Couscous-stuffed Poblano Peppers

Servings: 6
Cooking Time: 35 Minutes

Ingredients:

- 2 tablespoons olive oil
- ⅔ cup Israeli couscous
- 1 ¼ cups vegetable broth or water
- Kosher salt and freshly ground black pepper
- ½ medium onion, chopped
- 2 cloves garlic, minced
- 1 teaspoon dried oregano leaves
- ½ teaspoon ground cumin

- 1 (14.5-ounce) can fire-roasted diced tomatoes, with liquid
- Nonstick cooking spray
- 3 large poblano peppers, halved lengthwise, seeds and stem removed
- 1 ½ cups shredded Mexican blend, pepper Jack, or sharp cheddar cheese
- Optional toppings: minced fresh cilantro, sliced jalapeño peppers, diced tomatoes, sliced green onions (white and green portions)

Directions:

1. Heat 1 tablespoon oil in a medium saucepan over medium heat. Add the couscous and cook, stirring frequently, until golden brown, 2 to 3 minutes. Stir in the broth and season with salt and pepper. Cover, reduce the heat to a simmer, and cook, stirring occasionally, for about 10 minutes or until the liquid is absorbed. Remove from the heat and let stand, covered, for 5 minutes. Remove the cover, stir, and set aside to cool.

2. Heat the remaining 1 tablespoon oil in a small saucepan over medium heat. Add the onion, and cook, stirring frequently, for 3 to 5 minutes or until tender. Stir in the garlic and cook for 30 seconds. Stir in the oregano and cumin and season with salt and pepper. Stir in the tomatoes and simmer for 5 minutes.

3. Preheat the toaster oven to 400°F. Spray a 9-inch square baking pan with nonstick cooking spray. Spoon about one-third of the tomato mixture into the prepared pan. Arrange the peppers, cut side up, in the pan.

4. Stir 1 cup of the cheese into the couscous. Spoon the couscous mixture into the peppers, mounding slightly. Spoon the remaining tomato mixture over the peppers. Cover the pan and bake for 30 minutes.

5. Uncover the pan and sprinkle with the remaining cheese. Bake for 5 minutes or until the cheese is melted.

6. Top as desired with any of the various topping choices.

Chicken Marengo

Servings: 4
Cooking Time: 30 Minutes

Ingredients:

- Chicken mixture:
- 2 skinless, boneless chicken breast halves, cut into 1 × 1-inch pieces
- 6 large shrimp, peeled, deveined, and cut into 1 × 1-inch pieces
- 2 plum tomatoes, chopped
- 1 tablespoon olive oil
- ½ cup dry white wine
- 3 garlic cloves, chopped
- 6 fresh mushrooms, rinsed quickly, patted dry, and thinly sliced
- 1 teaspoon dried tarragon
- 1 tablespoon chopped fresh parsley
- Salt and freshly ground black pepper to taste
- 2 hard-boiled eggs, peeled and sliced
- ½ cup pitted and sliced black olives
- 2 tablespoons chopped fresh parsley

Directions:

1. Preheat the toaster oven to 375° F.

2. Combine the chicken mixture ingredients in a 1-quart 8½ × 8½ × 4-inch ovenproof baking dish and adjust the seasonings to taste. Cover with aluminum foil.

3. BAKE, covered, for 30 minutes, or until the chicken and shrimp are tender.

4. Garnish with slices of hard-boiled eggs, black olives, and parsley.

Creamy Roasted Pepper Basil Soup

Servings: 4

Cooking Time: 35 Minutes

Ingredients:

- 1 5-ounce jar roasted peppers, drained ½ cup fresh basil leaves
- 1 cup fat-free half-and-half
- 1 cup skim milk
- 2 tablespoons reduced-fat cream cheese
- 1 teaspoon garlic powder
- 1 teaspoon paprika
- Salt and freshly ground black pepper to taste
- 2 tablespoons chopped fresh basil leaves (garnish for cold soup)
- 2 tablespoons grated Parmesan cheese (topping for hot soup)

Directions:

1. Preheat the toaster oven to 400° F.

2. Process all the ingredients in a blender or food processor until smooth. Transfer the mixture to a 1-quart 8½ × 8½ × 4-inch ovenproof baking dish.

3. BAKE, covered, for 35 minutes. Ladle into individual soup bowls and serve.

Moroccan Couscous

Servings: 4   Cooking Time: 22 Minutes

Ingredients:

- 1 cup couscous
- 2 tablespoons finely chopped scallion
- 2 tablespoons finely chopped bell pepper
- 1 plum tomato, finely chopped
- 2 tablespoons chopped pitted black olives
- 1 tablespoon olive oil
- ¼ teaspoon ground cumin
- ¼ teaspoon ground cinnamon
- ¼ teaspoon turmeric Pinch of cayenne
- Salt and freshly ground black pepper to taste

Directions:

1. Preheat the toaster oven to 400° F.

2. Combine all the ingredients with ¼ cups water in a 1-quart 8½ × 8½ × 4-inch ovenproof baking dish. Adjust the seasonings to taste. Cover with aluminum foil.

3. BAKE, covered, for 12 minutes. Remove from the heat and fluff with a fork. Cover again and let stand for 10 minutes. Fluff once more before serving.

My Favorite Pizza

Servings: 4   Cooking Time: 30 Minutes

Ingredients:

- 1 9-inch ready-made pizza crust
- 1 8-ounce can tomato sauce
- 1 tablespoon olive oil
- 1 cup skinless, boneless chicken breast, cooked and cubed
- 3 plum tomatoes, chopped
- 1 bell pepper, quartered, seeded, and chopped
- 2 garlic cloves, minced
- ½ teaspoon dried oregano
- ½ teaspoon dried basil
- ½ teaspoon red pepper flakes
- 1 cup shredded part-skim, low-moisture mozzarella cheese

Directions:

1. Preheat the toaster oven to 400° F.

2. Spread the pizza crust with the tomato sauce. Drizzle with the olive oil and sprinkle with the chicken, tomatoes, pepper, garlic, seasonings, and cheese. Place the pizza on the toaster oven rack.

3. BAKE for 25 minutes, or until the topping is cooked and the crust is lightly browned.

Sheet Pan Loaded Nachos

Servings: 4

Cooking Time: 13 Minutes

Ingredients:

- 1 tablespoon canola or vegetable oil
- ½ pound lean ground beef
- ½ cup chopped onion
- 2 cloves garlic, minced
- 1 teaspoon chili powder
- ½ teaspoon ground cumin
- Kosher salt and freshly ground black pepper
- 6 ounces tortilla chips
- ½ cup canned black beans, rinsed and drained
- 1 ½ cups shredded sharp cheddar cheese or Mexican blend cheese
- ½ cup salsa
- Optional toppings: sliced jalapeño peppers, chopped bell peppers, sliced ripe olives, chopped tomatoes, minced fresh cilantro, sour cream, chopped avocado, guacamole, or chopped onion.

Directions:

1. Preheat the toaster oven to 400°F. Line a 12 x 12-inch baking pan with nonstick aluminum foil. (Or if lining the pan with regular foil, spray it with nonstick cooking spray.)

2. Heat the oil in a large skillet over medium-high heat. Add the ground beef and onion and cook, stirring frequently, until the beef is almost done. Add the garlic, chili powder, cumin, season with salt and pepper, and cook, stirring frequently, until the beef is fully cooked; drain.

3. Arrange the tortilla chips in an even layer in the prepared pan. Top with the beef-onion mixture, then top with the beans. Bake, uncovered, for 6 to 8 minutes. Top with the cheese and bake for 5 minutes more, or until the cheese is melted.

4. Drizzle with the salsa. Top as desired with any of the various toppings.

Salad Couscous

Servings: 4   Cooking Time: 10 Minutes

Ingredients:

- 1 10-ounce package precooked couscous
- 2 tablespoons olive oil
- Salt and freshly ground black pepper
- ¼ cup chopped fresh tomatoes
- 2 tablespoons chopped fresh basil leaves
- 1 tablespoon sliced almonds
- ½ bell pepper, chopped
- 3 scallions, chopped
- 2 tablespoons lemon juice

Directions:

1. Preheat the toaster oven to 400° F.

2. Mix together the couscous, 2 cups water, and olive oil in a 1-quart 8½ × 8½ × 4-inch ovenproof baking dish. Add salt and pepper to taste. Cover with aluminum foil.

3. BAKE, covered, for 10 minutes, or until the couscous is cooked. Remove from the oven, fluff with a fork and, when cool, add the tomatoes, basil leaves, almonds, pepper, scallions, and lemon juice. Adjust the seasonings to taste. Chill before serving.

One-step Classic Goulash

Servings: 4   Cooking Time: 56 Minutes

Ingredients:

- 1 cup elbow macaroni
- 1 cup (8-ounce can) tomato sauce
- 1 cup very lean ground round or sirloin
- 1 cup peeled and chopped fresh tomato
- ½ cup finely chopped onion
- 1 teaspoon garlic powder
- Salt and freshly ground black pepper
- Topping:
- 1 cup homemade bread crumbs
- 1 tablespoon margarine

Directions:

1. Preheat the toaster oven to 400° F.

2. Combine all the ingredients, except the topping, with 2 cups water in a 1-quart 8½ × 8½ × 4-inch ovenproof baking dish and mix well. Adjust the seasonings to taste. Cover with aluminum foil.

3. BAKE, covered, for 50 minutes, or until the macaroni is cooked, stirring after 25 minutes to distribute the liquid. Uncover, sprinkle with bread crumbs, and dot with margarine.

4. BROIL for 6 minutes, or until the topping is lightly browned.

Slow Cooker Chicken Philly Cheesesteak Sandwich

Servings: 4   Cooking Time: 2 Minutes

Ingredients:

- 1 3/4 to 2 pounds chicken tenders
- 2 large green peppers, cut in strips
- 2 medium onions, sliced
- 1 1/2 tablespoons rotisserie seasoning
- 1/2 teaspoon salt
- 4 tablespoons Italian salad dressing
- 4 hoagie rolls, split
- 4 slices Cheddar or American cheese
- 1/4 cup banana pepper rings, optional
- Hot Sauce or ketchup, optional

Directions:

1. In slow cooker crock, combine chicken tenders, pepper strips and onion slices with rotisserie seasoning and salt.

2. Cook on HIGH for 2 to 2 1/2 hours or LOW for 4 to 5 hours.

3. Preheat the toaster oven broiler. Open rolls and place on a cookie sheet

4. Slice chicken tenders. Place back in slow cooker. With a slotted spoon, divide chicken, peppers and onions among rolls and drizzle with Italian dressing. Top with cheese slices.

5. Place under broiler until cheese is melted, about 2 minutes.

6. Serve with banana peppers, hot sauce or ketchup, if desired.

Classic Beef Stew

Servings: 4   Cooking Time: 50 Minutes

Ingredients:

- 1½ cups dark beer
- 4 tablespoons unbleached flour
- 2 cups (approximately 1 pound) lean top round steak, cut into 1-inch cubes
- 1 cup peeled and coarsely chopped carrots
- 1 cup peeled and coarsely chopped potatoes
- ½ cup coarsely chopped onion
- 1 cup fresh or frozen peas
- 2 plum tomatoes, chopped
- 3 garlic cloves, minced
- 4 3 bay leaves
- ¼ teaspoon ground cumin
- Salt and butcher's pepper to taste

Directions:

1. Preheat the toaster oven to 400° F.

2. Whisk together the beer and flour in a 1-quart 8½ × 8½ × 4-inch ovenproof baking dish. Add all the other ingredients and seasonings and mix well, adjusting the seasonings to taste. Cover the dish with aluminum foil.

3. BAKE, covered, for 50 minutes, or until the meat is cooked and the vegetables are tender. Remove the bay leaves before serving.

Green Bean Soup

Servings: 4
Cooking Time: 47 Minutes

Ingredients:

- Roux mixture:
- 2 tablespoons unbleached flour
- 1 tablespoon margarine
- 3 cups water or low-sodium vegetable stock
- 1 cup (½ pound) fresh string beans, trimmed and cut into 1-inch pieces
- ½ teaspoon dried oregano
- ½ teaspoon ground cumin
- Salt and freshly ground black pepper to taste

Directions:

1. Combine the roux mixture in an 8½ × 8½ × 2-inch baking (cake) pan.

2. BROIL for 5 minutes, or until the margarine is melted. Remove from the oven and stir, then broil again for 2 minutes, or until the mixture is brown but not burned. Remove from the oven and stir to mix well. Set aside.

3. Combine the water or broth, string beans, and seasonings in a 1-quart 8½ × 8½ × 4-inch ovenproof baking dish. Stir in the roux mixture, blending well. Adjust the seasonings to taste.

4. BAKE, covered, at 375°F. for 40 minutes, or until the string beans are tender.

FISH AND SEAFOOD

Roasted Pepper Tilapia

Servings: 6
Cooking Time: 20 Minutes

Ingredients:

- 6 5-ounce tilapia fillets
- 2 tablespoons olive oil
- Filling:
- 1 cucumber, peeled, seeds scooped out and discarded, and chopped
- ½ cup chopped roasted peppers, drained
- 2 tablespoons lemon juice
- 2 tablespoons chopped fresh parsley or cilantro
- 1 teaspoon garlic powder
- 1 teaspoon paprika
- Salt and freshly ground black pepper to taste
- Dip mixture:
- 1 cup nonfat sour cream
- 2 tablespoons low-fat mayonnaise
- 3 tablespoons Dijon mustard
- 1 teaspoon Worcestershire sauce
- 1 teaspoon dried dill

Directions:

1. Combine the filling ingredients in a bowl, adjusting the seasonings to taste.

2. Spoon equal portions of filling in the centers of the tilapia filets. Roll up the fillets, starting at the smallest end. Secure each roll with toothpicks and place the rolls in an oiled or nonstick baking pan. Carefully brush the fillets with oil and place them in an oiled or nonstick 8½ × 8½ × 2-inch square baking (cake) pan.

3. BROIL for 20 minutes, or until the fillets are lightly browned. Combine the dip mixture ingredients in a small bowl and serve with the fish.

Popcorn Crawfish

Servings: 4
Cooking Time: 18 Minutes

Ingredients:

- ½ cup flour, plus 2 tablespoons
- ½ teaspoon garlic powder
- 1½ teaspoons Old Bay Seasoning
- ½ teaspoon onion powder
- ½ cup beer, plus 2 tablespoons
- 12-ounce package frozen crawfish tail meat, thawed and drained
- oil for misting or cooking spray
- Coating
- 1½ cups panko crumbs
- 1 teaspoon Old Bay Seasoning
- ½ teaspoon ground black pepper

Directions:

1. In a large bowl, mix together the flour, garlic powder, Old Bay Seasoning, and onion powder. Stir in beer to blend.

2. Add crawfish meat to batter and stir to coat.

3. Combine the coating ingredients in food processor and pulse to finely crush the crumbs. Transfer crumbs to shallow dish.

4. Preheat the toaster oven to 390°F.

5. Pour the crawfish and batter into a colander to drain. Stir with a spoon to drain excess batter.

6. Working with a handful of crawfish at a time, roll in crumbs and place on a cookie sheet. It's okay if some of the smaller pieces of crawfish meat stick together.

7. Spray breaded crawfish with oil or cooking spray and place all at once into air fryer oven.

8. Air-fry at 390°F for 5 minutes. Stir and mist again with olive oil or spray. Cook 5 more minutes, stir again, and mist lightly again. Continue cooking 5 more minutes, until browned and crispy.

Crispy Sweet-and-sour Cod Fillets

Servings: 3   Cooking Time: 12 Minutes

Ingredients:

- 1½ cups Plain panko bread crumbs (gluten-free, if a concern)
- 2 tablespoons Regular or low-fat mayonnaise (not fat-free; gluten-free, if a concern)
- ¼ cup Sweet pickle relish
- 3 4- to 5-ounce skinless cod fillets

Directions:

1. Preheat the toaster oven to 400°F.

2. Pour the bread crumbs into a shallow soup plate or a small pie plate. Mix the mayonnaise and relish in a small bowl until well combined. Smear this mixture all over the cod fillets. Set them in the crumbs and turn until evenly coated on all sides, even on the ends.

3. Set the coated cod fillets in the air fryer oven with as much air space between them as possible. They should not touch. Air-fry undisturbed for 12 minutes, or until browned and crisp.

4. Use a nonstick-safe spatula to transfer the cod pieces to a wire rack. Cool for only a minute or two before serving hot.

Scallops In Orange Sauce

Servings: 4   Cooking Time: 3 Minutes

Ingredients:

- Broiling mixture:
- 1 cup orange juice
- 1 teaspoon soy sauce
- 2 garlic cloves, finely minced
- 1 teaspoon grated orange zest
- 1½ pounds (3 cups) bay scallops, rinsed and drained
- 1 7-ounce can sliced water chestnuts, drained well
- 2 tablespoons chopped watercress

Directions:

1. Whisk together the broiling mixture ingredients in a small bowl and transfer to an 8½ × 8½ × 2-inch oiled or nonstick square (cake) pan.

2. BROIL the sauce for 10 minutes to reduce the liquid and meld the flavors. Remove the pan from the oven and add the scallops, spooning the sauce over them.

3. BROIL for 3 minutes, or until opaque. Serve the scallops with the sauce and garnish with the sliced water chestnuts and chopped watercress.

Horseradish Crusted Salmon

Servings: 2   Cooking Time: 14 Minutes

Ingredients:

- 2 (5-ounce) salmon fillets
- salt and freshly ground black pepper
- 2 teaspoons Dijon mustard
- ½ cup panko breadcrumbs
- 2 tablespoons prepared horseradish
- ½ teaspoon finely chopped lemon zest
- 1 tablespoon olive oil
- 1 tablespoon chopped fresh parsley

Directions:

1. Preheat the toaster oven to 360°F.

2. Season the salmon with salt and freshly ground black pepper. Then spread the Dijon mustard on the salmon, coating the entire surface.

3. Combine the breadcrumbs, horseradish, lemon zest and olive oil in a small bowl. Spread the mixture over the top of the salmon and press down lightly with your hands, adhering it to the salmon using the mustard as "glue".

4. Transfer the salmon to the air fryer oven and air-fry at 360°F for 14 minutes (depending on how thick your fillet is) or until the fish feels firm to the touch. Sprinkle with the parsley.

Stuffed Baked Red Snapper

Servings: 2   Cooking Time: 30 Minutes

Ingredients:

- Stuffing mixture:
- 12 medium shrimp, cooked, peeled, and chopped
- 2 tablespoons multigrain bread crumbs
- 1 teaspoon anchovy paste
- ¼ teaspoon paprika
- Salt to taste
- 2 6-ounce red snapper fillets
- 1 egg
- ½ cup fat-free half-and-half
- 2 tablespoons cooking sherry

Directions:

1. Preheat the toaster oven to 350° F.

2. Combine all the stuffing mixture ingredients in a medium bowl and place a mound of mixture on one end of each fillet. Fold over the other fillet end, skewering the edge with toothpicks.

3. Place the rolled fillets in an oiled or nonstick 8½ × 8½ × 2-inch square baking (cake) pan.

4. Whisk the egg in a small bowl until light in color, then whisk in the half-and-half and sherry. Pour over the fillets. Cover the pan with aluminum foil.

5. BAKE for 30 minutes.

Spicy Fish Street Tacos With Sriracha Slaw

Servings: 2   Cooking Time: 5 Minutes

Ingredients:

- Sriracha Slaw:
- ½ cup mayonnaise
- 2 tablespoons rice vinegar
- 1 teaspoon sugar
- 2 tablespoons sriracha chili sauce
- 5 cups shredded green cabbage
- ¼ cup shredded carrots
- 2 scallions, chopped
- salt and freshly ground black pepper
- Tacos:
- ½ cup flour
- 1 teaspoon chili powder
- ½ teaspoon ground cumin
- 1 teaspoon salt
- freshly ground black pepper
- ½ teaspoon baking powder
- 1 egg, beaten
- ¼ cup milk
- 1 cup breadcrumbs
- 1 pound mahi-mahi or snapper fillets
- 1 tablespoon canola or vegetable oil
- 6 (6-inch) flour tortillas
- 1 lime, cut into wedges

Directions:

1. Start by making the sriracha slaw. Combine the mayonnaise, rice vinegar, sugar, and sriracha sauce in a large bowl. Mix well and add the green cabbage, carrots, and scallions. Toss until all the vegetables are coated with the dressing and season with salt and pepper. Refrigerate the slaw until you are ready to serve the tacos.
2. Combine the flour, chili powder, cumin, salt, pepper and baking powder in a bowl. Add the egg and milk and mix until the batter is smooth. Place the breadcrumbs in shallow dish.
3. Cut the fish fillets into 1-inch wide sticks, approximately 4-inches long. You should have about 12 fish sticks total. Dip the fish sticks into the batter, coating all sides. Let the excess batter drip off the fish and then roll them in the breadcrumbs, patting the crumbs onto all sides of the fish sticks. Set the coated fish on a plate or baking sheet until all the fish has been coated.
4. Preheat the toaster oven to 400°F.
5. Spray the coated fish sticks with oil on all sides. Spray or brush the inside of the air fryer oven with oil and transfer the fish to the air fryer oven. Place as many sticks as you can in one layer, leaving a little room around each stick. Place any remaining sticks on top, perpendicular to the first layer.
6. Air-fry the fish for 3 minutes. Turn the fish sticks over and air-fry for an additional 2 minutes.
7. While the fish is air-frying, warm the tortilla shells either in a 350°F oven wrapped in foil or in a skillet with a little oil over medium-high heat for a couple minutes. Fold the tortillas in half and keep them warm until the remaining tortillas and fish are ready.
8. To assemble the tacos, place two pieces of the fish in each tortilla shell and top with the sriracha slaw. Squeeze the lime wedge over top and dig in.

Beer-breaded Halibut Fish Tacos

Servings: 4
Cooking Time: 10 Minutes

Ingredients:

- 1 pound halibut, cut into 1-inch strips
- 1 cup light beer
- 1 jalapeño, minced and divided
- 1 clove garlic, minced
- ¼ teaspoon ground cumin
- ½ cup cornmeal
- ¼ cup all-purpose flour
- 1¼ teaspoons sea salt, divided
- 2 cups shredded cabbage
- 1 lime, juiced and divided
- ¼ cup Greek yogurt
- ¼ cup mayonnaise
- 1 cup grape tomatoes, quartered
- ½ cup chopped cilantro
- ¼ cup chopped onion
- 1 egg, whisked
- 8 corn tortillas

Directions:

1. In a shallow baking dish, place the fish, the beer, 1 teaspoon of the minced jalapeño, the garlic, and the cumin. Cover and refrigerate for 30 minutes.

2. Meanwhile, in a medium bowl, mix together the cornmeal, flour, and ½ teaspoon of the salt.

3. In large bowl, mix together the shredded cabbage, 1 tablespoon of the lime juice, the Greek yogurt, the mayonnaise, and ½ teaspoon of the salt.

4. In a small bowl, make the pico de gallo by mixing together the tomatoes, cilantro, onion, ¼ teaspoon of the salt, the remaining jalapeño, and the remaining lime juice.

5. Remove the fish from the refrigerator and discard the marinade. Dredge the fish in the whisked egg; then dredge the fish in the cornmeal flour mixture, until all pieces of fish have been breaded.

6. Preheat the toaster oven to 350°F.

7. Place the fish in the air fryer oven and spray liberally with cooking spray. Air-fry for 6 minutes, flip the fish, and cook another 4 minutes.

8. While the fish is cooking, heat the tortillas in a heavy skillet for 1 to 2 minutes over high heat.

9. To assemble the tacos, place the battered fish on the heated tortillas, and top with slaw and pico de gallo. Serve immediately.

Shrimp, Chorizo And Fingerling Potatoes

Servings: 4
Cooking Time: 16 Minutes

Ingredients:

- ½ red onion, chopped into 1-inch chunks
- 8 fingerling potatoes, sliced into 1-inch slices or halved lengthwise
- 1 teaspoon olive oil
- salt and freshly ground black pepper
- 8 ounces raw chorizo sausage, sliced into 1-inch chunks
- 16 raw large shrimp, peeled, deveined and tails removed
- 1 lime
- ¼ cup chopped fresh cilantro
- chopped orange zest (optional)

Directions:

1. Preheat the toaster oven to 380°F.

2. Combine the red onion and potato chunks in a bowl and toss with the olive oil, salt and freshly ground black pepper.

3. Transfer the vegetables to the air fryer oven and air-fry for 6 minutes.

4. Add the chorizo chunks and continue to air-fry for another 5 minutes.

5. Add the shrimp, season with salt and continue to air-fry for another 5 minutes.

6. Transfer the tossed shrimp, chorizo and potato to a bowl and squeeze some lime juice over the top to taste. Toss in the fresh cilantro, orange zest and a drizzle of olive oil, and season again to taste.

7. Serve with a fresh green salad.

Baked Tomato Pesto Bluefish

Servings: 2   Cooking Time: 23 Minutes

Ingredients:

- 2 plum tomatoes
- 2 tablespoons tomato paste
- ¼ cup fresh basil leaves
- 1 tablespoon olive oil
- 2 garlic cloves
- 2 tablespoons pine nuts
- ¼ cup grated Parmesan cheese
- 1 teaspoon dried oregano
- Salt to taste
- 2 6-ounce bluefish fillets

Directions:

1. Preheat the toaster oven to 400° F.

2. Process the pesto ingredients in a blender or food processor until smooth.

3. Place the bluefish fillets in an oiled or nonstick 8½ × 8½ × 2-inch square baking (cake) pan.

4. BAKE, covered, for 15 minutes, or until the fish flakes with a fork. Remove from the oven, uncover, and spread the pesto mixture on both sides of the fillets.

5. BROIL, uncovered, for 8 minutes, or until the pesto is lightly browned.

Best-dressed Trout

Servings: 2   Cooking Time: 25 Minutes

Ingredients:

- 2 dressed trout
- 1 egg, beaten
- 2 tablespoons finely ground almonds
- 2 tablespoons unbleached flour
- 1 teaspoon paprika or smoked paprika
- Pinch of salt (optional)
- 4 lemon slices, approximately ¼ inch thick
- 1 teaspoon lemon juice

Directions:

1. Preheat the toaster oven to 400° F.

2. Brush the trout (both sides) with the beaten egg. Blend the almonds, flour, paprika, and salt in a bowl and sprinkle both sides of the trout. Insert 2 lemon slices in each trout cavity and place the trout in an oiled or nonstick 8½ × 8½ × 2-inch square baking (cake) pan.

3. BAKE for 20 minutes, or until the meat is white and firm. Remove from the oven and turn the trout carefully with a spatula.

4. BROIL for 5 minutes, or until the trout is lightly browned.

Shrimp With Jalapeño Dip

Servings: 4   Cooking Time: 10 Minutes

Ingredients:

- Seasonings:
- 1 teaspoon ground cumin
- 1 tablespoon minced garlic
- 1 teaspoon paprika
- 1 teaspoon chili powder
- Pinch of cayenne
- Salt to taste
- 1½ pounds large shrimp, peeled and deveined

Directions:

1. Combine the seasonings in a plastic bag, add the shrimp, and shake well to coat. Transfer the shrimp to an oiled or nonstick 8½ × 8½ × 2-inch square baking (cake) pan.

2. BROIL for 5 minutes. Remove the pan from the oven and turn the shrimp with tongs. Broil 5 minutes again, or until the shrimp are cooked (they should be firm but not rubbery.) Serve with Jalapeño Dip.

Shrimp Patties

Servings: 4   Cooking Time: 10 Minutes

Ingredients:

- ½ pound shelled and deveined raw shrimp
- ¼ cup chopped red bell pepper
- ¼ cup chopped green onion
- ¼ cup chopped celery
- 2 cups cooked sushi rice
- ½ teaspoon garlic powder
- ½ teaspoon Old Bay Seasoning
- ½ teaspoon salt
- 2 teaspoons Worcestershire sauce
- ½ cup plain breadcrumbs
- oil for misting or cooking spray

Directions:

1. Finely chop the shrimp. You can do this in a food processor, but it takes only a few pulses. Be careful not to overprocess into mush.

2. Place shrimp in a large bowl and add all other ingredients except the breadcrumbs and oil. Stir until well combined.

3. Preheat the toaster oven to 390°F.

4. Shape shrimp mixture into 8 patties, no more than ½-inch thick. Roll patties in breadcrumbs and mist with oil or cooking spray.

5. Place 4 shrimp patties in air fryer oven and air-fry at 390°F for 10 minutes, until shrimp cooks through and outside is crispy.

6. Repeat step 5 to cook remaining shrimp patties.

BEEF PORK AND LAMB

Easy Tex-mex Chimichangas

Servings: 2
Cooking Time: 8 Minutes

Ingredients:

- ¼ pound Thinly sliced deli roast beef, chopped
- ½ cup (about 2 ounces) Shredded Cheddar cheese or shredded Tex-Mex cheese blend
- ¼ cup Jarred salsa verde or salsa rojo
- ½ teaspoon Ground cumin
- ½ teaspoon Dried oregano
- 2 Burrito-size (12-inch) flour tortilla(s), not corn tortillas (gluten-free, if a concern)
- ⅔ cup Canned refried beans
- Vegetable oil spray

Directions:

1. Preheat the toaster oven to 375°F .

2. Stir the roast beef, cheese, salsa, cumin, and oregano in a bowl until well mixed.

3. Lay a tortilla on a clean, dry work surface. Spread ⅓ cup of the refried beans in the center lower third of the tortilla(s), leaving an inch on either side of the spread beans.

4. For one chimichanga, spread all of the roast beef mixture on top of the beans. For two, spread half of the roast beef mixture on each tortilla.

5. At either "end" of the filling mixture, fold the sides of the tortilla up and over the filling, partially covering it. Starting with the unfolded side of the tortilla just below the filling, roll the tortilla closed. Fold and roll the second filled tortilla, as necessary.

6. Coat the exterior of the tortilla(s) with vegetable oil spray. Set the chimichanga(s) seam side down in the air fryer oven, with at least ½ inch air space between them if you're working with two. Air-fry undisturbed for 8 minutes, or until the tortilla is lightly browned and crisp.

7. Use kitchen tongs to gently transfer the chimichanga(s) to a wire rack. Cool for at last 5 minutes or up to 20 minutes before serving.

Ribeye Steak With Blue Cheese Compound Butter

Servings: 2

Cooking Time: 12 Minutes

Ingredients:

- 5 tablespoons unsalted butter, softened
- ¼ cup crumbled blue cheese 2 teaspoons lemon juice
- 1 tablespoon freshly chopped chives
- Salt & freshly ground black pepper, to taste
- 2 (12 ounce) boneless ribeye steaks

Directions:

1. Mix together butter, blue cheese, lemon juice, and chives until smooth.

2. Season the butter to taste with salt and pepper.

3. Place the butter on plastic wrap and form into a 3-inch log, tying the ends of the plastic wrap together.

4. Place the butter in the fridge for 4 hours to harden.

5. Allow the steaks to sit at room temperature for 1 hour.

6. Pat the steaks dry with paper towels and season to taste with salt and pepper.

7. Insert the fry basket at top position in the Cosori Smart Air Fryer Toaster Oven.

8. Preheat the toaster Oven to 450°F.

9. Place the steaks in the fry basket in the preheated oven.

10. Select the Broil function, adjust time to 12 minutes, and press Start/Pause.

11. Remove when done and allow to rest for 5 minutes.

12. Remove the butter from the fridge, unwrap, and slice into ¾-inch pieces.

13. Serve the steak with one or two pieces of sliced compound butter.

Beef, Onion, And Pepper Shish Kebab

Servings: 4

Cooking Time: 20 Minutes

Ingredients:

- Marinade:
- 2 tablespoons olive oil
- ½ cup dry red wine
- 1 tablespoon soy sauce
- 1 teaspoon chili powder
- 1 teaspoon Worcestershire sauce
- 1 teaspoon garlic powder
- 1 teaspoon spicy brown mustard
- 1 teaspoon brown sugar
- 8 onion quarters, approximately 2 × 2-inch pieces
- 8 bell pepper quarters, 2 × 2-inch pieces
- 1 pound lean boneless beef (sirloin, round steak, London broil), cut into 8 2-inch cubes
- 4 8-inch metal or wooden (bamboo) skewers

Directions:

1. Combine the marinade ingredients in a large bowl. Add the onion, peppers, and beef. Refrigerate, covered, for at least 1 hour or

2. Skewer alternating beef, pepper, and onion pieces. Brush with the marinade mixture and place the skewers on a broiling rack with the pan underneath.

3. BROIL for 5 minutes, remove the pan with the skewers from the oven, turn the skewers, brush again, then broil for another 5 minutes. Repeat turning and brushing every 5 minutes, until the peppers and onions are well cooked and browned to your preference.

Barbeque Ribs

Servings: 4
Cooking Time: 35 Minutes

Ingredients:

- 2 pounds pork spareribs or baby back ribs, silver skin removed
- 2 tablespoons brown sugar
- 1 teaspoon chili powder
- 1 teaspoon dry mustard
- Sea salt, for seasoning
- Freshly ground black pepper, for seasoning
- Oil spray (hand-pumped)
- 1 cup barbeque sauce

Directions:

1. Preheat the toaster oven to 375°F on AIR FRY for 5 minutes.

2. Cut the ribs into 4 bone sections or to fit in the basket.

3. In a small bowl, combine the brown sugar, chili powder, and mustard, and rub it all over the ribs.

4. Season the ribs with salt and pepper.

5. Place the air-fryer basket in the baking tray and spray it generously with the oil.

6. Arrange the ribs in the basket. There can be overlap if necessary.

7. In position 2, air fry for 35 minutes, turning halfway through, until the ribs are tender, browned, and crisp.

8. Baste the ribs with the barbeque sauce and serve.

Vietnamese Beef Lettuce Wraps

Servings: 4

Cooking Time: 12 Minutes

Ingredients:

- ⅓ cup low-sodium soy sauce
- 2 teaspoons fish sauce
- 2 teaspoons brown sugar
- 1 tablespoon chili paste
- juice of 1 lime
- 2 cloves garlic, minced
- 2 teaspoons fresh ginger, minced
- 1 pound beef sirloin
- Sauce
- ⅓ cup low-sodium soy sauce

- juice of 2 limes
- 1 tablespoon mirin wine
- 2 teaspoons chili paste
- Serving
- 1 head butter lettuce
- ½ cup julienned carrots
- ½ cup julienned cucumber
- ½ cup sliced radishes, sliced into half moons
- 2 cups cooked rice noodles
- ⅓ cup chopped peanuts

Directions:

1. Combine the soy sauce, fish sauce, brown sugar, chili paste, lime juice, garlic and ginger in a bowl. Slice the beef into thin slices, then cut those slices in half. Add the beef to the marinade and marinate for 1 to 3 hours in the refrigerator. When you are ready to cook, remove the steak from the refrigerator and let it sit at room temperature for 30 minutes.

2. Preheat the toaster oven to 400°F.

3. Transfer the beef and marinade to the air fryer oven. Air-fry at 400°F for 12 minutes.

4. While the beef is cooking, prepare a wrap-building station. Combine the soy sauce, lime juice, mirin wine and chili paste in a bowl and transfer to a little pouring vessel. Separate the lettuce leaves from the head of lettuce and put them in a serving bowl. Place the carrots, cucumber, radish, rice noodles and chopped peanuts all in separate serving bowls.

5. When the beef has finished cooking, transfer it to another serving bowl and invite your guests to build their wraps. To build the wraps, place some beef in a lettuce leaf and top with carrots, cucumbers, some rice noodles and chopped peanuts. Drizzle a little sauce over top, fold the lettuce around the ingredients and enjoy!

Perfect Strip Steaks

Servings: 2

Cooking Time: 17 Minutes

Ingredients:

- 1½ tablespoons Olive oil
- 1½ tablespoons Minced garlic
- 2 teaspoons Ground black pepper
- 1 teaspoon Table salt
- 2 ¾-pound boneless beef strip steak(s)

Directions:

1. Preheat the toaster oven to 375°F (or 380°F or 390°F, if one of these is the closest setting).

2. Mix the oil, garlic, pepper, and salt in a small bowl, then smear this mixture over both sides of the steak(s).

3. When the machine is at temperature, put the steak(s) in the air fryer oven with as much air space as possible between them for the larger batch. They should not overlap or even touch. That said, even just a ¼-inch between them will work. Air-fry for 12 minutes, turning once, until an instant-read meat thermometer inserted into the thickest part of a steak registers 127°F for rare (not USDA-approved). Or air-fry for 15 minutes, turning once, until an instant-read meat thermometer registers 145°F for medium (USDA-approved). If the machine is at 390°F, the steaks may cook 2 minutes more quickly than the stated timing.

4. Use kitchen tongs to transfer the steak(s) to a wire rack. Cool for 5 minutes before serving.

Tuscan Pork Tenderloin

Servings: 4

Cooking Time: 35 Minutes

Ingredients:

- Nonstick cooking spray.
- 1 pork tenderloin (1 ¼ to 1 ½ pounds)
- Kosher salt and freshly ground black pepper
- 8 to 10 fresh basil leaves
- 1 ½ teaspoons minced garlic (about 3 cloves garlic)
- 2 slices prosciutto
- 2 ounces mozzarella cheese, cut into thin strips, or ½ cup shredded
- 1 tablespoon olive oil
- 1 teaspoon Italian seasoning

Directions:

1. Preheat the toaster oven to 400°F. Spray a 12 x 12-inch baking pan with nonstick cooking spray.

2. Cut the pork tenderloin in half lengthwise, not quite cutting through one side, and gently open it (like a book) so it lays flat. Cover the meat with plastic wrap. Pound the meat with the flat side of a meat pounder until the meat is even and about ½ inch thick.

3. Season the cut side of the meat with salt and pepper. Arrange the basil leaves evenly over the meat, then sprinkle with 1 teaspoon of the minced garlic. Top with an even layer of prosciutto and cheese. Roll the meat from the longer side covering the cheese and other filling ingredients completely. Tie the meat shut with kitchen twine, taking care to keep the roll tight and the filling inside.

4. Rub the outside of the meat with the olive oil. Mix the Italian seasoning and the remaining ½ teaspoon garlic in a small bowl. Season with salt and pepper. Rub the seasoning mixture evenly over the meat.

5. Place the meat in the prepared pan. Roast, uncovered, for 25 to 35 minutes or until the tenderloin is brown and the pork is just slightly pink inside.

6. Let stand for 5 to 10 minutes. Slice crosswise into slices about 1 inch thick.

Better-than-chinese-take-out Pork Ribs

Servings: 3

Cooking Time: 35 Minutes

Ingredients:

- 1½ tablespoons Hoisin sauce (gluten-free, if a concern)
- 1½ tablespoons Regular or low-sodium soy sauce or gluten-free tamari sauce
- 1½ tablespoons Shaoxing (Chinese cooking rice wine), dry sherry, or white grape juice
- 1½ teaspoons Minced garlic
- ¾ teaspoon Ground dried ginger
- ¾ teaspoon Ground white pepper
- 1½ pounds Pork baby back rib rack(s), cut into 2-bone pieces

Directions:

1. Mix the hoisin sauce, soy or tamari sauce, Shaoxing or its substitute, garlic, ginger, and white pepper in a large bowl. Add the rib sections and stir well to coat. Cover and refrigerate for at least 2 hours or up to 24 hours, stirring the rib sections in the marinade occasionally.

2. Preheat the toaster oven to 350°F . Set the ribs in their bowl on the counter as the machine heats.

3. When the machine is at temperature, set the rib pieces on their sides in a single layer in the air fryer oven with as much air space between them as possible. Air-fry for 35 minutes, turning and rearranging the pieces once, until deeply browned and sizzling.

4. Use kitchen tongs to transfer the rib pieces to a large serving bowl or platter. Wait a minute or two before serving them so the meat can reabsorb some of its own juices.

Spicy Little Beef Birds

Servings: 2

Cooking Time: 12 Minutes

Ingredients:

- Spicy mixture:
- 1 tablespoon olive oil
- 1 tablespoon brown mustard
- 1 teaspoon chili powder
- 1 teaspoon garlic powder
- 1 teaspoon hot sauce
- 1 tablespoon barbecue sauce or salsa
- Salt and freshly ground black pepper to taste
- ½ to ¾ pound pepper steaks, cut into 3 × 4-inch strips

Directions:

1. Blend the spicy mixture ingredients in a small bowl and brush both sides of the beef strips.

2. Roll up the strips lengthwise and fasten with toothpicks near each end. Place the beef rolls in an oiled or nonstick 8½ × 8½ × 2-inch square baking (cake) pan.

3. BROIL for 6 minutes, remove from the oven, and turn with tongs. Brush with the spicy mixture and broil again for 6 minutes, or until done to your preference.

Stuffed Bell Peppers

Servings: 4
Cooking Time: 10 Minutes

Ingredients:

- ¼ pound lean ground pork
- ¾ pound lean ground beef
- ¼ cup onion, minced
- 1 15-ounce can Red Gold crushed tomatoes
- 1 teaspoon Worcestershire sauce
- 1 teaspoon barbeque seasoning
- 1 teaspoon honey
- ½ teaspoon dried basil
- ½ cup cooked brown rice
- ½ teaspoon garlic powder
- ½ teaspoon oregano
- ½ teaspoon salt
- 2 small bell peppers

Directions:

1. Place pork, beef, and onion in air fryer oven baking pan and air-fry at 360°F for 5 minutes.

2. Stir to break apart chunks and cook 3 more minutes. Continue cooking and stirring in 2-minute intervals until meat is well done. Remove from pan and drain.

3. In a small saucepan, combine the tomatoes, Worcestershire, barbeque seasoning, honey, and basil. Stir well to mix in honey and seasonings.

4. In a large bowl, combine the cooked meat mixture, rice, garlic powder, oregano, and salt. Add ¼ cup of the seasoned crushed tomatoes. Stir until well mixed.

5. Cut peppers in half and remove stems and seeds.

6. Stuff each pepper half with one fourth of the meat mixture.

7. Place the peppers in air fryer oven and air-fry for 10 minutes, until peppers are crisp tender.

8. Heat remaining tomato sauce. Serve peppers with warm sauce spooned over top.

Lamb Curry

Servings: 4
Cooking Time: 40 Minutes

Ingredients:

- 1 pound lean lamb for stewing, trimmed and cut into 1 × 1-inch pieces
- 1 small onion, chopped
- 3 garlic cloves, minced
- 2 plum tomatoes, chopped
- ½ cup dry white wine
- 2 tablespoons curry powder
- Salt and cayenne to taste

Directions:

1. Preheat the toaster oven to 400° F.

2. Combine all the ingredients in an 8½ × 8½ × 4-inch ovenproof baking dish. Adjust the seasonings.

3. BAKE, covered, for 40 minutes, or until the meat is tender and the onion is cooked.

Smokehouse-style Beef Ribs

Servings: 3
Cooking Time: 25 Minutes

Ingredients:

- ¼ teaspoon Mild smoked paprika
- ¼ teaspoon Garlic powder
- ¼ teaspoon Ground black pepper
- 3 10- to 12-ounce beef back ribs (not beef short ribs)
- ¼ teaspoon Onion powder
- ¼ teaspoon Table salt

Directions:

1. Preheat the toaster oven to 350°F .

2. Mix the smoked paprika, garlic powder, onion powder, salt, and pepper in a small bowl until uniform. Massage and pat this mixture onto the ribs.

3. When the machine is at temperature, set the ribs in the air fryer oven in one layer, turning them on their sides if necessary, sort of like they're spooning but with at least ¼ inch air space between them. Air-fry for 25 minutes, turning once, until deep brown and sizzling.

4. Use kitchen tongs to transfer the ribs to a wire rack. Cool for 5 minutes before serving.

Glazed Meatloaf

Servings: 4
Cooking Time: 60 Minutes

Ingredients:

- 2 pounds extra-lean ground beef
- ½ cup fine bread crumbs
- 1 large egg
- 1 medium carrot, shredded
- 2 teaspoons minced garlic
- ¼ cup milk
- 1 tablespoon Italian seasoning
- ½ teaspoon sea salt
- ⅛ teaspoon freshly ground black pepper
- ½ cup ketchup
- 1 tablespoon dark brown sugar
- 1 teaspoon apple cider vinegar

Directions:

1. Place the rack in position 1 and preheat the toaster oven to 375°F on BAKE for 5 minutes.

2. In a large bowl, mix the ground beef, bread crumbs, egg, carrot, garlic, milk, Italian seasoning, salt, and pepper until well combined.

3. Press the mixture into a 9-by-5-inch loaf pan.

4. In a small bowl, stir the ketchup, brown sugar, and vinegar. Set aside.

5. Bake for 40 minutes.

6. Take the meatloaf out and spread the glaze over the top. Bake an additional 20 minutes until cooked through, with an internal temperature of 165°F. Serve.

I Forgot To Thaw—garlic Capered Chicken Thighs

Servings: 4

Cooking Time: 50 Minutes

Ingredients:

- 6 frozen skinless, boneless chicken thighs
- Garlic mixture:
- 3 garlic cloves, minced
- ¾ cup dry white wine
- 2 tablespoons capers
- ½ teaspoon paprika
- ¼ teaspoon ground cumin
- Salt and freshly ground black pepper to taste

Directions:

1. Preheat the toaster oven to 400° F.

2. Thaw the chicken as directed. Separate the pieces and add the garlic mixture, which has been combined in a small bowl, stirring well to coat. Cover the dish with aluminum foil.

3. BAKE for 30 minutes, or until the chicken is tender. Remove the cover and turn the chicken pieces, spooning the sauce over them.

4. BROIL for 8 minutes, or until the chicken is lightly browned.

Golden Seasoned Chicken Wings

Servings: 2

Cooking Time: 40 Minutes

Ingredients:

- Oil spray (hand-pumped)
- ¾ cup all-purpose flour
- 1 teaspoon garlic powder
- 1 teaspoon smoked paprika
- ½ teaspoon sea salt
- ¼ teaspoon freshly ground black pepper
- ¼ teaspoon onion powder
- 2 pounds chicken wing drumettes and flats

Directions:

1. Preheat the toaster oven to 400°F on AIR FRY for 5 minutes.

2. Place the air-fryer basket in the baking tray and spray it generously with the oil.

3. In a medium bowl, stir the flour, garlic powder, paprika, sea salt, pepper, and onion powder until well mixed.

4. Add half the chicken wings to the bowl and toss to coat with the flour.

5. Arrange the wings in the basket and spray both sides lightly with the oil.

6. In position 2, air fry for 20 minutes, turning halfway through, until golden brown and crispy.

7. Repeat with the remaining wings, covering the cooked wings loosely with foil to keep them warm. Serve.

Nacho Chicken Fries

Servings: 4
Cooking Time: 7 Minutes

Ingredients:

- 1 pound chicken tenders
- salt
- ¼ cup flour
- 2 eggs
- ¾ cup panko breadcrumbs
- ¾ cup crushed organic nacho cheese tortilla chips
- oil for misting or cooking spray
- Seasoning Mix
- 1 tablespoon chili powder
- 1 teaspoon ground cumin
- ½ teaspoon garlic powder
- ½ teaspoon onion powder

Directions:

1. Stir together all seasonings in a small cup and set aside.

2. Cut chicken tenders in half crosswise, then cut into strips no wider than about ½ inch.

3. Preheat the toaster oven to 390°F.

4. Salt chicken to taste. Place strips in large bowl and sprinkle with 1 tablespoon of the seasoning mix. Stir well to distribute seasonings.

5. Add flour to chicken and stir well to coat all sides.

6. Beat eggs together in a shallow dish.

7. In a second shallow dish, combine the panko, crushed chips, and the remaining 2 teaspoons of seasoning mix.

8. Dip chicken strips in eggs, then roll in crumbs. Mist with oil or cooking spray.

9. Chicken strips will cook best if done in two batches. They can be crowded and overlapping a little but not stacked in double or triple layers.

10. Air-fry for 4 minutes. Mist with oil, and cook 3 more minutes, until chicken juices run clear and outside is crispy.

11. Repeat step 10 to cook remaining chicken fries.

Curry Powder

Servings: 1

Cooking Time: 5 Minutes

Ingredients:

- ½ cup coriander seeds
- 2 tablespoons ground cumin
- 2 tablespoons black peppercorns
- 1 tablespoon sesame seeds
- 1 tablespoon cardamom seeds, extracted from the pods
- 2 small dried chili peppers
- 3 tablespoons turmeric
- 2 tablespoons ground ginger

Directions:

1. Combine the coriander seeds, cumin, peppercorns, sesame seeds, cardamom seeds, and chili peppers in an oiled or nonstick 8½ × 8½ × 2-inch square baking (cake) pan.

2. TOAST once, then turn with tongs and toast again, or continue toasting and turning until evenly toasted. Cool and grind the spices in a blender until the mixture becomes a powder. Add the turmeric and ground ginger and mix well. Store in a covered container in the refrigerator.

Chicken Parmesan

Servings: 4
Cooking Time: 11 Minutes

Ingredients:

- 4 chicken tenders
- Italian seasoning
- salt
- ¼ cup cornstarch
- ½ cup Italian salad dressing
- ¼ cup panko breadcrumbs
- ¼ cup grated Parmesan cheese, plus more for serving
- oil for misting or cooking spray
- 8 ounces spaghetti, cooked
- 1 24-ounce jar marinara sauce

Directions:

1. Pound chicken tenders with meat mallet or rolling pin until about ¼-inch thick.

2. Sprinkle both sides with Italian seasoning and salt to taste.

3. Place cornstarch and salad dressing in 2 separate shallow dishes.

4. In a third shallow dish, mix together the panko crumbs and Parmesan cheese.

5. Dip flattened chicken in cornstarch, then salad dressing. Dip in the panko mixture, pressing into the chicken so the coating sticks well.

6. Spray both sides with oil or cooking spray. Place in air fryer oven in single layer.

7. Air-fry at 390°F for 5 minutes. Spray with oil again, turning chicken to coat both sides. See tip about turning.

8. Air-fry for an additional 6 minutes or until chicken juices run clear and outside is browned.

9. While chicken is cooking, heat marinara sauce and stir into cooked spaghetti.

10. To serve, divide spaghetti with sauce among 4 dinner plates, and top each with a fried chicken tender. Pass additional Parmesan at the table for those who want extra cheese.

Chicken Souvlaki Gyros

Servings: 4
Cooking Time: 18 Minutes

Ingredients:

- ¼ cup extra-virgin olive oil
- 1 clove garlic, crushed
- 1 tablespoon Italian seasoning
- ½ teaspoon paprika
- ½ lemon, sliced
- ¼ teaspoon salt
- 1 pound boneless, skinless chicken breasts
- 4 whole-grain pita breads
- 1 cup shredded lettuce
- ½ cup chopped tomatoes
- ¼ cup chopped red onion
- ¼ cup cucumber yogurt sauce

Directions:

1. In a large resealable plastic bag, combine the olive oil, garlic, Italian seasoning, paprika, lemon, and salt. Add the chicken to the bag and secure shut. Vigorously shake until all the ingredients are combined. Set in the fridge for 2 hours to marinate.

2. When ready to cook, preheat the toaster oven to 360°F.

3. Liberally spray the air fryer oven with olive oil mist. Remove the chicken from the bag and discard the leftover marinade. Place the chicken into the air fryer oven, allowing enough room between the chicken breasts to flip.

4. Air-fry for 10 minutes, flip, and cook another 8 minutes.

5. Remove the chicken from the air fryer oven when it has cooked (or the internal temperature of the chicken reaches 165°F). Let rest 5 minutes. Then thinly slice the chicken into strips.

6. Assemble the gyros by placing the pita bread on a flat surface and topping with chicken, lettuce, tomatoes, onion, and a drizzle of yogurt sauce.

7. Serve warm.

Chicken Wellington

Servings: 4   Cooking Time: 30 Minutes

Ingredients:

- 2 small (5- to 6-ounce) boneless, skinless chicken breast halves
- Kosher salt and freshly ground black pepper
- 2 teaspoons Italian seasoning
- 2 tablespoons olive oil
- 3 tablespoons unsalted butter, softened
- 3 ounces cream cheese, softened (about ⅓ cup)
- ¾ cup shredded Monterey Jack cheese
- ¼ cup grated Parmesan cheese
- 1 cup frozen (loose-pack) chopped spinach, thawed and squeezed dry
- ¾ cup chopped canned artichoke hearts, drained
- ½ teaspoon garlic powder
- 1 sheet frozen puff pastry, about 9 inches square, thawed (½ of a 17.3-ounce package)
- 1 large egg, lightly beaten

Directions:

1. Preheat the toaster oven to 425° F. Line a 12 x 12-inch baking pan with parchment paper.

2. Cut the chicken breasts in half lengthwise. Season each piece with the salt, pepper, and Italian seasoning. Fold the thinner end under the larger piece to make the chicken breasts into a rounded shape. Secure with toothpicks.

3. Heat a large skillet over medium-high heat. Add the olive oil and heat. Add the chicken breasts and brown well, turning to brown evenly. Remove from the skillet and set aside to cool. Remove the toothpicks.

4. Stir the butter, cream cheese, Monterey Jack, and Parmesan in a large bowl. Stir in the spinach, artichoke hearts, and garlic powder. Season with salt and pepper.

5. Roll out the puff pastry sheet on a lightly floured board until it makes a 12-inch square. Cut into four equal pieces. Spread one-fourth of the spinach-artichoke mixture on the surface of each pastry square to within ½ inch of all four edges. Place the chicken in the center of each. Gently fold the puff pastry up over the chicken and pinch the edges to seal tightly.

6. Place each chicken bundle, seam side down, on the prepared pan. Brush the top of each bundle lightly with the beaten egg. Bake for 25 to 30 minutes, or until the pastry is golden brown and crisp and a meat thermometer inserted into the chicken reaches 165°F.

Chicken Chunks

Servings: 4
Cooking Time: 10 Minutes

Ingredients:

- 1 pound chicken tenders cut in large chunks, about 1½ inches
- salt and pepper
- ½ cup cornstarch
- 2 eggs, beaten
- 1 cup panko breadcrumbs
- oil for misting or cooking spray

Directions:

1. Season chicken chunks to your liking with salt and pepper.

2. Dip chicken chunks in cornstarch. Then dip in egg and shake off excess. Then roll in panko crumbs to coat well.

3. Spray all sides of chicken chunks with oil or cooking spray.

4. Place chicken in air fryer oven in single layer and air-fry at 390°F for 5 minutes. Spray with oil, turn chunks over, and spray other side.

5. Air-fry for an additional 5 minutes or until chicken juices run clear and outside is golden brown.

6. Repeat steps 4 and 5 to cook remaining chicken.

Jerk Chicken Drumsticks

Servings: 2
Cooking Time: 20 Minutes

Ingredients:

- 1 or 2 cloves garlic
- 1 inch of fresh ginger
- 2 serrano peppers, (with seeds if you like it spicy, seeds removed for less heat)
- 1 teaspoon ground allspice
- 1 teaspoon ground nutmeg
- 1 teaspoon chili powder
- ½ teaspoon dried thyme
- ½ teaspoon ground cinnamon
- ½ teaspoon paprika
- 1 tablespoon brown sugar
- 1 teaspoon soy sauce
- 2 tablespoons vegetable oil
- 6 skinless chicken drumsticks

Directions:

1. Combine all the ingredients except the chicken in a small chopper or blender and blend to a paste. Make slashes into the meat of the chicken drumsticks and rub the spice blend all over the chicken (a pair of plastic gloves makes this really easy). Transfer the rubbed chicken to a non-reactive covered container and let the chicken marinate for at least 30 minutes or overnight in the refrigerator.

2. Preheat the toaster oven to 400°F.

3. Transfer the drumsticks to the air fryer oven. Air-fry for 10 minutes. Turn the drumsticks over and air-fry for another 10 minutes. Serve warm with some rice and vegetables or a green salad.

Hot Thighs

Servings: 4
Cooking Time: 40 Minutes

Ingredients:

- 6 skinless, boneless chicken thighs
- ¼ cup fresh lemon juice
- Seasonings:
- 1 teaspoon garlic powder
- ¼ teaspoon cayenne
- ½ teaspoon chili powder
- 1 teaspoon onion powder
- Salt and freshly ground black pepper to taste

Directions:

1. Preheat the toaster oven to 450° F.

2. Brush the chicken thighs liberally with the lemon juice. Set aside.

3. Combine the seasonings in a small bowl and transfer to a paper or plastic bag. Add the thighs and shake well to coat. Remove from the bag and place in an oiled or nonstick 8½ × 8½ × 2-inch square (cake) pan. Cover the pan with aluminum foil.

4. BAKE, covered, for 20 minutes. Turn the pieces with tongs and bake again for another 20 minutes, or until the meat is tender and lightly browned.

Crispy Chicken Parmesan

Servings: 4
Cooking Time: 12 Minutes

Ingredients:

- 4 skinless, boneless chicken breasts, pounded thin to ¼-inch thickness
- 1 teaspoon salt, divided
- ½ teaspoon black pepper, divided
- 1 cup flour
- 2 eggs
- 1 cup panko breadcrumbs
- ½ teaspoon dried oregano
- ½ cup grated Parmesan cheese

Directions:

1. Pat the chicken breasts with a paper towel. Season the chicken with ½ teaspoon of the salt and ¼ teaspoon of the pepper.

2. In a medium bowl, place the flour.

3. In a second bowl, whisk the eggs.

4. In a third bowl, place the breadcrumbs, oregano, cheese, and the remaining ½ teaspoon of salt and ¼ teaspoon of pepper.

5. Dredge the chicken in the flour and shake off the excess. Dip the chicken into the eggs and then into the breadcrumbs. Set the chicken on a plate and repeat with the remaining chicken pieces.

6. Preheat the toaster oven to 360°F.

7. Place the chicken in the air fryer oven and spray liberally with cooking spray. Air-fry for 8 minutes, turn the chicken breasts over, and cook another 4 minutes. When golden brown, check for an internal temperature of 165°F.

Sweet-and-sour Chicken

Servings: 6
Cooking Time: 10 Minutes

Ingredients:

- 1 cup pineapple juice
- 1 cup plus 3 tablespoons cornstarch, divided
- ¼ cup sugar
- ¼ cup ketchup
- ¼ cup apple cider vinegar
- 2 tablespoons soy sauce or tamari
- 1 teaspoon garlic powder, divided
- ¼ cup flour
- 1 tablespoon sesame seeds
- ½ teaspoon salt
- ¼ teaspoon ground black pepper
- 2 large eggs
- 2 pounds chicken breasts, cut into 1-inch cubes
- 1 red bell pepper, cut into 1-inch pieces
- 1 carrot, sliced into ¼-inch-thick rounds

Directions:

1. In a medium saucepan, whisk together the pineapple juice, 3 tablespoons of the cornstarch, the sugar, the ketchup, the apple cider vinegar, the soy sauce or tamari, and ½ teaspoon of the garlic powder. Cook over medium-low heat, whisking occasionally as the sauce thickens, about 6 minutes. Stir and set aside while preparing the chicken.

2. Preheat the toaster oven to 370°F.

3. In a medium bowl, place the remaining 1 cup of cornstarch, the flour, the sesame seeds, the salt, the remaining ½ teaspoon of garlic powder, and the pepper.

4. In a second medium bowl, whisk the eggs.

5. Working in batches, place the cubed chicken in the cornstarch mixture to lightly coat; then dip it into the egg mixture, and return it to the cornstarch mixture. Shake off the excess and place the coated chicken in the air fryer oven. Spray with cooking spray and air-fry for 5 minutes, and spray with more cooking spray. Cook an additional 3 to 5 minutes, or until completely cooked and golden brown.

6. On the last batch of chicken, add the bell pepper and carrot to the air fryer oven and cook with the chicken.

7. Place the cooked chicken and vegetables into a serving bowl and toss with the sweet-and-sour sauce to serve.

VEGETABLES AND VEGETARIAN

Potato Skins

Servings: 4   Cooking Time: 20 Minutes

Ingredients:

- 4 potato shells

Directions:

1. Place 4 potato shells in an oiled or nonstick 8½ × 8½ × 2-inch square baking (cake) pan.

2. Brush, sprinkle, and fill with a variety of seasonings or ingredients.

3. BROIL 20 minutes, or until browned and crisped to your preference.

Five-spice Roasted Sweet Potatoes

Servings: 4   Cooking Time: 12 Minutes

Ingredients:

- ½ teaspoon ground cinnamon
- ¼ teaspoon ground cumin
- ¼ teaspoon paprika
- 1 teaspoon chile powder
- ⅛ teaspoon turmeric
- ½ teaspoon salt (optional)
- freshly ground black pepper
- 2 large sweet potatoes, peeled and cut into ¾-inch cubes (about 3 cups)
- 1 tablespoon olive oil

Directions:

1. In a large bowl, mix together cinnamon, cumin, paprika, chile powder, turmeric, salt, and pepper to taste.

2. Add potatoes and stir well.

3. Drizzle the seasoned potatoes with the olive oil and stir until evenly coated.

4. Place seasoned potatoes in the air fryer oven baking pan or an ovenproof dish that fits inside your air fryer oven.

5. Air-fry for 6 minutes at 390°F, stop, and stir well.

6. Air-fry for an additional 6 minutes.

Latkes

Servings: 12
Cooking Time: 13 Minutes

Ingredients:

- 1 russet potato
- ¼ onion
- 2 eggs, lightly beaten
- ⅓ cup flour
- ½ teaspoon baking powder
- 1 teaspoon salt
- freshly ground black pepper
- canola or vegetable oil, in a spray bottle
- chopped chives, for garnish
- apple sauce
- sour cream

Directions:

1. Shred the potato and onion with a coarse box grater or a food processor with the shredding blade. Place the shredded vegetables into a colander or mesh strainer and squeeze or press down firmly to remove the excess water.

2. Transfer the onion and potato to a large bowl and add the eggs, flour, baking powder, salt and black pepper. Mix to combine and then shape the mixture into patties, about ¼-cup of mixture each. Brush or spray both sides of the latkes with oil.

3. Preheat the toaster oven to 400°F.

4. Air-fry the latkes in batches. Transfer one layer of the latkes to the air fryer oven and air-fry at 400°F for 12 to 13 minutes, flipping them over halfway through the cooking time. Transfer the finished latkes to a platter and cover with aluminum foil, or place them in a warm oven to keep warm.

5. Garnish the latkes with chopped chives and serve with sour cream and applesauce.

Crispy Herbed Potatoes

Servings: 6
Cooking Time: 20 Minutes

Ingredients:

- 3 medium baking potatoes, washed and cubed
- ½ teaspoon dried thyme
- 1 teaspoon minced dried rosemary
- ½ teaspoon garlic powder
- 1 teaspoon sea salt
- ½ teaspoon black pepper
- 2 tablespoons extra-virgin olive oil
- ¼ cup chopped parsley

Directions:

1. Preheat the toaster oven to 390°F.

2. Pat the potatoes dry. In a large bowl, mix together the cubed potatoes, thyme, rosemary, garlic powder, sea salt, and pepper. Drizzle and toss with olive oil.

3. Pour the herbed potatoes into the air fryer oven. Air-fry for 20 minutes, stirring every 5 minutes.

4. Toss the cooked potatoes with chopped parsley and serve immediately.

5. VARY IT! Potatoes are versatile — add any spice or seasoning mixture you prefer and create your own favorite side dish.

Lemon-glazed Baby Carrots

Servings: 4
Cooking Time: 33 Minutes

Ingredients:

- Glaze:
- 1 tablespoon margarine
- 2 tablespoons lemon juice
- 1 tablespoon honey
- 1 teaspoon garlic powder
- Salt and freshly ground black pepper to taste
- 2 cups peeled baby carrots (approximately 1 pound)
- 1 tablespoon chopped fresh parsley or cilantro

Directions:

1. Place the glaze ingredients in a 1-quart 8½ × 8½ × 4-inch ovenproof baking dish and broil for 4 minutes, or until the margarine is melted. Remove from the oven and mix well. Add the carrots and toss to coat. Cover the dish with aluminum foil.

2. BAKE, covered, at 350° F. for 30 minutes, or until the carrots are tender. Garnish with chopped parsley or cilantro and serve immediately.

Crispy, Cheesy Leeks

Servings: 4

Cooking Time: 15 Minutes

Ingredients:

- 2 Medium leek(s), about 9 ounces each
- Olive oil spray
- ¼ cup Seasoned Italian-style dried bread crumbs (gluten-free, if a concern)
- ¼ cup (about ¾ ounce) Finely grated Parmesan cheese
- 2 tablespoons Olive oil

Directions:

1. Preheat the toaster oven to 350°F .

2. Trim off the root end of the leek(s) as well as the dark green top(s), leaving about a 5-inch usable section. Split the leek section(s) in half lengthwise. Set the leek halves cut side up on your work surface. Pull out and remove in one piece the semicircles that make up the inner structure of the leek, about halfway down. Set the removed "inside" next to the outer leek "shells" on your cutting board. Generously coat them all on all sides (particularly the "bottoms") with olive oil spray.

3. Set the leeks and their insides cut side up in the air fryer oven with as much air space between them as possible. Air-fry undisturbed for 12 minutes.

4. Meanwhile, mix the bread crumbs, cheese, and olive oil in a small bowl until well combined.

5. After 12 minutes in the air fryer oven, sprinkle this mixture inside the leek shells and on top of the leek insides. Increase the machine's temperature to 375°F (or 380°F or 390°F, if one of these is the closest setting). Air-fry undisturbed for 3 minutes, or until the topping is lightly browned.

6. Use a nonstick-safe spatula to transfer the leeks to a serving platter. Cool for a few minutes before serving warm.

Ratatouille

Servings: 4
Cooking Time: 60 Minutes

Ingredients:

- Oil spray (hand-pumped)
- 1 eggplant, peeled and diced into ½-inch chunks
- 2 tomatoes, diced
- 1 zucchini, diced
- 2 bell peppers (any color), diced
- ½ red onion, chopped
- ½ cup tomato paste
- 2 teaspoons minced garlic
- 1 teaspoon dried basil
- ¼ teaspoon sea salt
- ⅛ teaspoon freshly ground black pepper
- Pinch red pepper flakes
- ½ cup low-sodium vegetable broth

Directions:

1. Place the rack in position 1 and preheat oven to 350°F on CONVECTION BAKE for 5 minutes.

2. Lightly coat a 1½-quart casserole dish with oil spray.

3. In a large bowl, toss the eggplant, tomatoes, zucchini, bell peppers, onion, tomato paste, garlic, basil, salt, black pepper, and red pepper flakes until well combined.

4. Transfer the vegetable mixture to the casserole dish, pour in the vegetable broth, and cover tightly with foil or a lid.

5. Convection bake for 1 hour, stirring once at the halfway mark, until the vegetables are very tender. Serve.

Mashed Potato Tots

Servings: 18
Cooking Time: 10 Minutes

Ingredients:
- 1 medium potato or 1 cup cooked mashed potatoes
- 1 tablespoon real bacon bits
- 2 tablespoons chopped green onions, tops only
- ¼ teaspoon onion powder
- 1 teaspoon dried chopped chives
- salt
- 2 tablespoons flour
- 1 egg white, beaten
- ½ cup panko breadcrumbs
- oil for misting or cooking spray

Directions:
1. If using cooked mashed potatoes, jump to step 4.

2. Peel potato and cut into ½-inch cubes. (Small pieces cook more quickly.) Place in saucepan, add water to cover, and heat to boil. Lower heat slightly and continue cooking just until tender, about 10 minutes.

3. Drain potatoes and place in ice cold water. Allow to cool for a minute or two, then drain well and mash.

4. Preheat the toaster oven to 390°F.

5. In a large bowl, mix together the potatoes, bacon bits, onions, onion powder, chives, salt to taste, and flour. Add egg white and stir well.

6. Place panko crumbs on a sheet of wax paper.

7. For each tot, use about 2 teaspoons of potato mixture. To shape, drop the measure of potato mixture onto panko crumbs and push crumbs up and around potatoes to coat edges. Then turn tot over to coat other side with crumbs.

8. Mist tots with oil or cooking spray and place in air fryer oven, crowded but not stacked.

9. Air-fry at 390°F for 10 minutes, until browned and crispy.

10. Repeat steps 8 and 9 to cook remaining tots.

Homemade Potato Puffs

Servings: 4
Cooking Time: 15 Minutes

Ingredients:

- 1¾ cups Water
- 4 tablespoons (¼ cup/½ stick) Butter
- 2 cups plus 2 tablespoons Instant mashed potato flakes
- 1½ teaspoons Table salt
- ¾ teaspoon Ground black pepper
- ¼ teaspoon Mild paprika
- ¼ teaspoon Dried thyme
- 1¼ cups Seasoned Italian-style dried bread crumbs (gluten-free, if a concern)
- Olive oil spray

Directions:

1. Heat the water with the butter in a medium saucepan set over medium-low heat just until the butter melts. Do not bring to a boil.

2. Remove the saucepan from the heat and stir in the potato flakes, salt, pepper, paprika, and thyme until smooth. Set aside to cool for 5 minutes.

3. Preheat the toaster oven to 400°F. Spread the bread crumbs on a dinner plate.

4. Scrape up 2 tablespoons of the potato flake mixture and form it into a small, oblong puff, like a little cylinder about 1½ inches long. Gently roll the puff in the bread crumbs until coated on all sides. Set it aside and continue making more, about 12 for the small batch, 18 for the medium batch, or 24 for the large.

5. Coat the potato cylinders with olive oil spray on all sides, then arrange them in the air fryer oven in one layer with some air space between them. Air-fry undisturbed for 15 minutes, or until crisp and brown.

6. Gently dump the contents of the air fryer oven onto a wire rack. Cool for 5 minutes before serving.

Zucchini Fries

Servings: 3
Cooking Time: 12 Minutes

Ingredients:

- 1 large Zucchini
- ½ cup All-purpose flour or tapioca flour
- 2 Large egg(s), well beaten
- 1 cup Seasoned Italian-style dried bread crumbs (gluten-free, if a concern)
- Olive oil spray

Directions:

1. Preheat the toaster oven to 400°F.

2. Trim the zucchini into a long rectangular block, taking off the ends and four "sides" to make this shape. Cut the block lengthwise into ½-inch-thick slices. Lay these slices flat and cut in half widthwise. Slice each of these pieces into ½-inch-thick batons.

3. Set up and fill three shallow soup plates or small pie plates on your counter: one for the flour, one for the beaten egg(s), and one for the bread crumbs.

4. Set a zucchini baton in the flour and turn it several times to coat all sides. Gently stir any excess flour, then dip it in the egg(s), turning it to coat. Let any excess egg slip back into the rest, then set the baton in the bread crumbs and turn it several times, pressing gently to coat all sides, even the ends. Set aside on a cutting board and continue coating the remainder of the batons in the same way.

5. Lightly coat the batons on all sides with olive oil spray. Set them in two flat layers in the air fryer oven, the top layer at a 90-degree angle to the bottom one, with a little air space between the batons in each layer. In the end, the whole thing will look like a crosshatch pattern. Air-fry undisturbed for 6 minutes.

6. Use kitchen tongs to gently rearrange the batons so that any covered parts are now uncovered. The batons no longer need to be in a crosshatch pattern. Continue air-frying undisturbed for 6 minutes, or until lightly browned and crisp.

7. Gently pour the contents of the air fryer oven onto a wire rack. Spread the batons out and cool for only a minute or two before serving.

Roasted Garlic

Servings: 1
Cooking Time: 20 Minutes

Ingredients:

- 3 whole garlic buds
- 3 tablespoons olive oil
- Salt and freshly ground black pepper

Directions:

1. Preheat the toaster oven to 450° F.

2. Place the garlic buds in an oiled or nonstick 8½ × 8½ × 2-inch square baking (cake) pan.

3. BAKE, uncovered, for 20 minutes, or until the buds are tender when pierced with a skewer or sharp knife. When cool enough to handle, peel and mash the baked cloves with a fork into the olive oil. Season with salt and pepper to taste.

Buttery Rolls

Servings: 6   Cooking Time: 14 Minutes

Ingredients:

- 6½ tablespoons Room-temperature whole or low-fat milk
- 3 tablespoons plus 1 teaspoon Butter, melted and cooled
- 3 tablespoons plus 1 teaspoon (or 1 medium egg, well beaten) Pasteurized egg substitute, such as Egg Beaters
- 1½ tablespoons Granulated white sugar
- 1¼ teaspoons Instant yeast
- ¼ teaspoon Table salt
- 2 cups, plus more for dusting All-purpose flour
- Vegetable oil
- Additional melted butter, for brushing

Directions:

1. Stir the milk, melted butter, pasteurized egg substitute (or whole egg), sugar, yeast, and salt in a medium bowl to combine. Stir in the flour just until the mixture makes a soft dough.

2. Lightly flour a clean, dry work surface. Turn the dough out onto the work surface. Knead the dough for 5 minutes to develop the gluten.

3. Lightly oil the inside of a clean medium bowl. Gather the dough into a compact ball and set it in the bowl. Turn the dough over so that its surface has oil on it all over. Cover the bowl tightly with plastic wrap and set aside in a warm, draft-free place until the dough has doubled in bulk, about 1½ hours.

4. Punch down the dough, then turn it out onto a clean, dry work surface. Divide it into 5 even balls for a small batch, 6 balls for a medium batch, or 8 balls for a large one.

5. For a small batch, lightly oil the inside of a 6-inch round cake pan and set the balls around its perimeter, separating them as much as possible.

6. For a medium batch, lightly oil the inside of a 7-inch round cake pan and set the balls in it with one ball at its center, separating them as much as possible.

7. For a large batch, lightly oil the inside of an 8-inch round cake pan and set the balls in it with one at the center, separating them as much as possible.

8. Cover with plastic wrap and set aside to rise for 30 minutes.

9. Preheat the toaster oven to 350°F .

10. Uncover the pan and brush the rolls with a little melted butter, perhaps ½ teaspoon per roll. When the machine is at temperature, set the cake pan in the air fryer oven. Air-fry undisturbed for 14 minutes, or until the rolls have risen and browned.

11. Using kitchen tongs and a nonstick-safe spatula, two hot pads, or silicone baking mitts, transfer the cake pan from the air fryer oven to a wire rack. Cool the rolls in the pan for a minute or two. Turn the rolls out onto a wire rack, set them top side up again, and cool for at least another couple of minutes before serving warm.

DESSERTS

Carrot Cake

Servings: 6
Cooking Time: 30 Minutes

Ingredients:

FOR THE CAKE

- ½ cup canola oil, plus extra for greasing the baking dish
- 1 cup all-purpose flour, plus extra for dusting the baking dish
- 1 cup granulated sugar
- 1 teaspoon baking powder
  FOR THE ICING
- 4 ounces cream cheese, room temperature
- ¼ cup salted butter, room temperature

- ½ teaspoon sea salt
- 2 teaspoons pumpkin pie spice
- 2 large eggs
- 1 cup carrot, finely shredded
- ½ cup dried apricot, chopped

- 1 teaspoon vanilla extract
- 2 cups confectioners' sugar

Directions:

1. To make the cake

2. Place the rack in position 1 and preheat the oven to 325°F on BAKE for 5 minutes.

3. Lightly grease an 8-inch-square baking dish with oil and dust with flour.

4. Place the rack in position 1.

5. In a large bowl, stir the flour, sugar, baking powder, salt, and pumpkin pie spice.

6. Make a well in the center and add the oil and eggs, stirring until just combined. Add the carrot and apricot and stir until well mixed.

7. Transfer the batter to the baking dish and bake for about 30 minutes until golden brown and a toothpick inserted in the center comes out clean.

8. Remove the cake from the oven and cool completely in the baking dish.

9. To make the icing

10. When the cake is cool, whisk the cream cheese, butter, and vanilla until very smooth and blended. Add the confectioners' sugar and whisk until creamy and thick, about 2 minutes.

11. Ice the cake and serve.

Chocolate Caramel Pecan Cupcakes

Servings: 6
Cooking Time: 20 Minutes

Ingredients:

- 6 tablespoons all-purpose flour
- 6 tablespoons unsweetened cocoa powder
- ¼ teaspoon baking soda
- ¼ teaspoon baking powder
- ⅛ teaspoon table salt
- 6 tablespoons unsalted butter, softened
- ½ cup granulated sugar
- 1 large egg
- ½ teaspoon pure vanilla extract
- ½ cup sour cream
- BUTTERCREAM FROSTING
- ¼ cup unsalted butter, softened
- 1 ¾ cups confectioners' sugar
- 2 to 3 tablespoons half and half or milk
- 1 teaspoon pure vanilla extract
- Caramel ice cream topping
- ¼ cup caramelized chopped pecans

Directions:

1. Preheat the toaster oven to 350°F. Line a 6-cup muffin pan with cupcake papers.

2. Whisk the flour, cocoa, baking soda, baking powder, and salt in a small bowl; set aside.

3. Beat the butter and granulated sugar in a large bowl with a handheld mixer at medium-high speed for 2 minutes, or until the mixture is light and creamy. Beat in the egg well. Beat in the vanilla.

4. On low speed, beat in the flour mixture in thirds, alternating with the sour cream, beginning and ending with the flour mixture. The batter will be thick.

5. Spoon the batter evenly into the prepared cupcake cups, filling each about three-quarters full. Bake for 18 to 20 minutes, or until a wooden pick inserted into the center comes out clean. Place on a wire rack and let cool completely.

6. Meanwhile, make the frosting: Beat the butter in a large bowl using a handheld mixer on medium-high speed until creamy. Gradually beat in the confectioners' sugar. Beat in 2 tablespoons of half-and-half and the vanilla. Beat in the remaining tablespoon of half-and-half, as needed, until the frosting is of desired consistency.

7. Frost each cooled cupcake. Drizzle the caramel topping in thin, decorative stripes over the frosting. Top with the caramelized pecans.

Almond-roasted Pears

Servings: 4

Cooking Time: 15 Minutes

Ingredients:

- Yogurt Topping
- 1 container vanilla Greek yogurt (5–6 ounces)
- ¼ teaspoon almond flavoring
- 2 whole pears
- ¼ cup crushed Biscoff cookies (approx. 4 cookies)
- 1 tablespoon sliced almonds
- 1 tablespoon butter

Directions:

1. Stir almond flavoring into yogurt and set aside while preparing pears.

2. Halve each pear and spoon out the core.

3. Place pear halves in air fryer oven.

4. Stir together the cookie crumbs and almonds. Place a quarter of this mixture into the hollow of each pear half.

5. Cut butter into 4 pieces and place one piece on top of crumb mixture in each pear.

6. Preheat the toaster oven to 400°F and air-fry for 15 minutes or until pears have cooked through but are still slightly firm.

7. Serve pears warm with a dollop of yogurt topping.

Black And Blue Clafoutis

Servings: 2

Cooking Time: 15 Minutes

Ingredients:

- 6-inch pie pan
- 3 large eggs
- ½ cup sugar
- 1 teaspoon vanilla extract
- 2 tablespoons butter, melted 1 cup milk
- ½ cup all-purpose flour
- 1 cup blackberries
- 1 cup blueberries
- 2 tablespoons confectioners' sugar

Directions:

1. Preheat the toaster oven to 320°F.

2. Combine the eggs and sugar in a bowl and whisk vigorously until smooth, lighter in color and well combined. Add the vanilla extract, butter and milk and whisk together well. Add the flour and whisk just until no lumps or streaks of white remain.

3. Scatter half the blueberries and blackberries in a greased (6-inch) pie pan or cake pan. Pour half of the batter (about 1¼ cups) on top of the berries and transfer the tart pan to the air fryer oven. You can use an aluminum foil sling to help with this by taking a long piece of aluminum foil, folding it in half lengthwise twice until it is roughly 26-inches by 3-inches. Place this under the pie dish and hold the ends of the foil to move the pie dish in and out of the air fryer oven. Tuck the ends of the foil beside the pie dish while it cooks in the air fryer oven.

4. Air-fry at 320°F for 15 minutes or until the clafoutis has puffed up and is still a little jiggly in the center. Remove the clafoutis from the air fryer oven, invert it onto a plate and let it cool while you bake the second batch. Serve the clafoutis warm, dusted with confectioners' sugar on top.

Donut Holes

Servings: 13
Cooking Time: 12 Minutes

Ingredients:

- 6 tablespoons Granulated white sugar
- 1½ tablespoons Butter, melted and cooled
- 2 tablespoons (or 1 small egg, well beaten) Pasteurized egg substitute, such as Egg Beaters
- 6 tablespoons Regular or low-fat sour cream (not fat-free)
- ¾ teaspoon Vanilla extract
- 1⅔ cups All-purpose flour
- ¾ teaspoon Baking powder
- ¼ teaspoon Table salt
- Vegetable oil spray

Directions:

1. Preheat the toaster oven to 350°F .

2. Whisk the sugar and melted butter in a medium bowl until well combined. Whisk in the egg substitute or egg , then the sour cream and vanilla until smooth. Remove the whisk and stir in the flour, baking powder, and salt with a wooden spoon just until a soft dough forms.

3. Use 2 tablespoons of this dough to create a ball between your clean palms. Set it aside and continue making balls: 8 more for the small batch, 12 more for the medium batch, or 17 more for the large one.

4. Coat the balls in the vegetable oil spray, then set them in the air fryer oven with as much air space between them as possible. Even a fraction of an inch will be enough, but they should not touch. Air-fry undisturbed for 12 minutes, or until browned and cooked through. A toothpick inserted into the center of a ball should come out clean.

5. Pour the contents of the air fryer oven onto a wire rack. Cool for at least 5 minutes before serving.

Blueberry Cheesecake Tartlets

Servings: 9
Cooking Time: 6 Minutes

Ingredients:

- 8 ounces cream cheese, softened
- ¼ cup sugar
- 1 egg
- ½ teaspoon vanilla extract
- zest of 2 lemons, divided
- 9 mini graham cracker tartlet shells
- 2 cups blueberries
- ½ teaspoon ground cinnamon
- juice of ½ lemon
- ¼ cup apricot preserves

Directions:

1. Preheat the toaster oven to 330°F.

2. Combine the cream cheese, sugar, egg, vanilla and the zest of one lemon in a medium bowl and blend until smooth by hand or with an electric hand mixer. Pour the cream cheese mixture into the tartlet shells.

3. Air-fry 3 tartlets at a time at 330°F for 6 minutes, rotating them in the air fryer oven halfway through the cooking time.

4. Combine the blueberries, cinnamon, zest of one lemon and juice of half a lemon in a bowl. Melt the apricot preserves in the microwave or over low heat in a saucepan. Pour the apricot preserves over the blueberries and gently toss to coat.

5. Allow the cheesecakes to cool completely and then top each one with some of the blueberry mixture. Garnish the tartlets with a little sugared lemon peel and refrigerate until you are ready to serve.

Heavenly Chocolate Cupcakes

Servings: 6
Cooking Time: 30 Minutes

Ingredients:

- 2 squares semisweet chocolate
- 2 tablespoons margarine
- 1 cup unbleached flour
- 2 teaspoons baking powder
- Salt to taste
- ¾ cup brown sugar
- ½ cup skim milk
- 1 egg, beaten
- ½ cup chopped pecans
- ½ teaspoon vanilla extract

Directions:

1. Melt the chocolate and margarine in an oiled or nonstick 8½ × 8½ × 2-inch square baking (cake) pan under the broiler for 5 minutes, or until about half melted. Remove from the oven and stir until completely melted and blended.

2. Combine the flour, baking powder, salt, and sugar in a medium bowl, mixing well. Add the melted chocolate/margarine mixture, then the milk and egg. Stir to blend well, then stir in the pecans and vanilla. Fill paper baking cups or well-oiled tins in a 6-muffin pan three-quarters full with batter.

3. BAKE at 350° F. for 25 minutes, or until a toothpick inserted in the center comes out clean.

Sweet Potato Donut Holes

Servings: 18
Cooking Time: 4 Minutes

Ingredients:

- 1 cup flour
- ⅓ cup sugar
- ¼ teaspoon baking soda
- 1 teaspoon baking powder
- ⅛ teaspoon salt
- ½ cup cooked mashed purple sweet potatoes
- 1 egg, beaten
- 2 tablespoons butter, melted
- 1 teaspoon pure vanilla extract
- oil for misting or cooking spray

Directions:

1. Preheat the toaster oven to 390°F.

2. In a large bowl, stir together the flour, sugar, baking soda, baking powder, and salt.

3. In a separate bowl, combine the potatoes, egg, butter, and vanilla and mix well.

4. Add potato mixture to dry ingredients and stir into a soft dough.

5. Shape dough into 1½-inch balls. Mist lightly with oil or cooking spray.

6. Place 9 donut holes in air fryer oven, leaving a little space in between. Air-fry for 4 minutes, until done in center and lightly browned outside.

7. Repeat step 6 to cook remaining donut holes.

Goat Cheese–stuffed Nectarines

Servings: 4
Cooking Time: 10 Minutes

Ingredients:

- 4 ripe nectarines, halved and pitted
- 1 tablespoon olive oil
- 1 cup soft goat cheese, room temperature
- 1 tablespoon maple syrup
- ¼ teaspoon vanilla extract
- ¼ teaspoon ground cinnamon
- 2 tablespoons pecans, chopped

Directions:

1. Preheat the toaster oven to 350°F on AIR FRY for 5 minutes.

2. Place the air-fryer basket in the baking tray and place the nectarines in the basket, hollow-side up. Brush the tops and hollow of the fruit with the olive oil.

3. In position 2, air fry for 5 minutes to soften and lightly brown the fruit.

4. While the fruit is air frying, in a small bowl, stir the goat cheese, maple syrup, vanilla, and cinnamon until well blended.

5. Take the fruit out and evenly divide the cheese filling between the halves. Air fry for 5 minutes until the filling is heated through and a little melted.

6. Serve topped with pecans.

Baked Custard

Servings: 2
Cooking Time: 45 Minutes

Ingredients:

- 2 eggs
- ¼ cup sugar
- 1 cup low-fat evaporated milk
- ½ teaspoon vanilla extract
- Pinch of grated nutmeg
- Fat-free half-and-half

Directions:

1. Preheat the toaster oven to 350° F.

2. Beat together the eggs, sugar, milk, vanilla, and nutmeg in a small bowl with an electric mixer at medium speed. Pour equal portions of the custard mixture into 2 oiled 1-cup-size ovenproof dishes.

3. BAKE for 45 minutes, or until a toothpick inserted in the center comes out clean. Serve drizzled with warm fat-free half-and-half.

Orange-glazed Brownies

Servings: 12

Cooking Time: 30 Minutes

Ingredients:

- 3 squares unsweetened chocolate
- 3 tablespoons margarine
- 1 cup sugar
- ½ cup orange juice
- 2 eggs
- 1½ cups unbleached flour
- 1 teaspoon baking powder
- Salt to taste
- 1 tablespoon grated orange zest
- Orange Glaze (recipe follows)

Directions:

1. BROIL the chocolate and margarine in an oiled or nonstick 8½ × 8½ × 2-inch square baking (cake) pan for 3 minutes, or until almost melted. Remove from the oven and stir until completely melted. Transfer the chocolate/margarine mixture to a medium bowl.

2. Beat in the sugar, orange juice, and eggs with an electric mixer. Stir in the flour, baking powder, salt, and orange zest and mix until well blended. Pour into the oiled or nonstick square cake pan.

3. BAKE at 350° F. for 30 minutes, or until a toothpick inserted in the center comes out clean. Make holes over the entire top by piercing with a fork or toothpick. Paint with Orange Glaze and cut into squares.

Apple Strudel

Servings: 2
Cooking Time: 90 Minutes

Ingredients:

- 2 Golden Delicious apples (14 ounces), peeled, cored, and cut into ½-inch pieces
- 1½ tablespoons granulated sugar
- ¼ teaspoon grated lemon zest plus 1 teaspoon juice
- ⅛ teaspoon ground cinnamon
- ⅛ tcaspoon ground gingcr
- ⅛ teaspoon table salt, divided
- 2 tablespoons golden raisins
- 1 tablespoon panko bread crumbs
- 3½ tablespoons unsalted butter, melted
- 1½ teaspoons confectioners' sugar, plus extra for serving
- 7 (14 by 9-inch) phyllo sheets, thawed

Directions:

1. Toss apples, granulated sugar, lemon zest and juice, cinnamon, ginger, and pinch salt together in large bowl. Cover and microwave until apples are softened, 2 to 4 minutes, stirring once halfway through microwaving. Let apples sit, covered, for 5 minutes. Transfer apples to colander set in second large bowl and let drain, reserving liquid. Return apples to bowl; stir in raisins and panko.

2. Adjust toaster oven rack to middle position and preheat the toaster oven to 350 degrees. Spray small rimmed baking sheet with vegetable oil spray. Stir remaining pinch salt into melted butter.

3. Place 16½ by 12-inch sheet of parchment paper on counter with long side parallel to edge of counter. Place 1 phyllo sheet on parchment with long side parallel to edge of counter. Place confectioners' sugar in fine-mesh strainer. Lightly brush sheet with melted butter and dust sparingly with confectioners' sugar. Repeat with remaining 6 phyllo sheets, melted butter, and confectioners' sugar, stacking sheets one on top of other as you go.

4. Arrange apple mixture in 2½ by 10-inch rectangle 2 inches from bottom of phyllo and about 2 inches from each side. Using parchment, fold sides of phyllo over filling, then fold bottom edge of phyllo over filling. Brush folded portions of phyllo with reserved apple liquid. Fold top edge over filling, making sure top and bottom edges overlap by about 1 inch. (If they do not overlap, unfold, rearrange filling into slightly narrower strip, and refold.) Press firmly to seal. Using thin metal spatula, transfer strudel to prepared sheet. Lightly brush top and sides of strudel with remaining apple liquid.

5. Bake until golden brown, 25 to 30 minutes, rotating sheet halfway through baking. Using thin metal spatula, immediately transfer strudel to cutting board. Let cool for 3 minutes. Slice strudel and let cool for at least 20 minutes. Serve warm or at room temperature, dusting with extra confectioners' sugar before serving.

Fried Pickles

Servings: 2
Cooking Time: 15 Minutes

Ingredients:

- 1 egg
- 1 tablespoon milk
- ¼ teaspoon hot sauce
- 2 cups sliced dill pickles, well drained
- ¾ cup breadcrumbs
- oil for misting or cooking spray

Directions:

1. Preheat the toaster oven to 390°F.

2. Beat together egg, milk, and hot sauce in a bowl large enough to hold all the pickles.

3. Add pickles to the egg wash and stir well to coat.

4. Place breadcrumbs in a large plastic bag or container with lid.

5. Drain egg wash from pickles and place them in bag with breadcrumbs. Shake to coat.

6. Pile pickles into air fryer oven and spray with oil.

7. Air-fry for 5 minutes. Spray with oil.

8. Cook 5 more minutes. Shake and spray again. Separate any pickles that have stuck together and mist any spots you've missed.

9. Air-fry for 5 minutes longer or until dark golden brown and crispy.

Potato Samosas

Servings: 12

Cooking Time: 10 Minutes

Ingredients:
- ¾ cup Instant mashed potato flakes
- ¾ cup Boiling water
- ⅓ cup Plain full-fat or low-fat yogurt (not Greek yogurt or fat-free yogurt)
- 1 teaspoon Yellow curry powder, purchased or homemade
- ½ teaspoon Table salt
- 1½ Purchased refrigerated pie crust(s), from a minimum 14.1-ounce box
- All-purpose flour
- Vegetable oil spray

Directions:

1. Put the potato flakes in a medium bowl and pour the boiling water over them. Stir well to form a mixture like thick mashed potatoes. Cool for 15 minutes.

2. Preheat the toaster oven to 400°F.

3. Stir the yogurt, curry powder, and salt into the potato mixture until smooth and uniform.

4. Unwrap and unroll the sheet(s) of pie crust dough onto a clean, dry work surface. Cut out as many 4-inch circles as you can with a big cookie cutter or a giant sturdy water glass, or even by tracing the circle with the rim of a 4-inch plate. Gather up the scraps of dough. Lightly flour your work surface and set the scraps on top. Roll them together into a sheet that matches the thickness of the original crusts and cut more circles until you have the number you need—8 circles for the small batch, 12 for the medium batch, or 16 for the large.

5. Pick up one of the circles and create something like an ice cream cone by folding and sealing the circle together so that it is closed at the bottom and flared open at the top, in a conical shape. Put 1 tablespoon of the potato filling into the open cone, then push the filling into the cone toward the point. Fold the top over the filling and press to seal the dough into a triangular shape with corners, taking care to seal those corners all around. Set aside and continue forming and filling the remainder of the dough circles as directed.

6. Lightly coat the filled dough pockets with vegetable oil spray on all sides. Set them in the air fryer oven in one layer and air-fry undisturbed for 10 minutes, or until lightly browned and crisp.

7. Gently turn the contents of the air fryer oven out onto a wire rack. Use kitchen tongs to gently set all the samosas seam side up. Cool for 10 minutes before serving.

Rosemary Roasted Vegetables

Servings: 4
Cooking Time: 25 Minutes

Ingredients:

- 3 tablespoons olive oil
- Grated zest and juice of 1 lemon
- 2 tablespoons chopped fresh rosemary leaves
- 4 cloves garlic, minced
- Kosher salt and freshly ground black pepper
- 6 cups vegetables, diced, such as bell peppers, onions, zucchini, mushrooms, cherry tomatoes, potatoes, and eggplant

Directions:

1. Preheat the toaster oven to 425 °F.

2. Stir the olive oil, lemon zest, lemon juice, rosemary, and garlic in a small bowl. Season with salt and pepper. Place the vegetables into a large bowl and drizzle the olive oil mixture over all. Stir gently to coat.

3. Arrange the vegetables in a single layer in a 12 x 12-inch baking pan. Roast for 10 minutes. Stir and roast for an additional 10 to 15 minutes, or until the vegetables are tender.

Creamy Scalloped Potatoes

Servings: 4
Cooking Time: 58 Minutes

Ingredients:

- Oil spray (hand-pumped)
- 2 tablespoons salted butter
- 1 small onion, finely chopped
- 1 teaspoon minced garlic
- 2 tablespoons all-purpose flour
- 1 cup whole milk
- ½ cup low-sodium chicken broth
- ¼ teaspoon ground nutmeg
- ⅛ teaspoon sea salt
- ⅛ teaspoon freshly ground black pepper
- 1½ pounds russet potatoes, cut into ⅛-inch-thick slices

Directions:

1. Place the rack on position 1 and preheat the toaster oven on BAKE to 350°F for 5 minutes.

2. Lightly spray an 8-inch-square baking dish with oil and set aside.

3. Melt the butter in a medium saucepan over medium-high heat. Sauté the onion and garlic in the butter until softened, about 4 minutes. Add the flour and cook, whisking, for 1 minute.

4. Whisk in the milk and chicken broth until well blended and cook, whisking constantly, until thickened, about 3 minutes. Remove the sauce from the heat and whisk in the nutmeg, salt, and pepper. Set aside.

5. Layer one-third of the potato slices in the baking dish and top with one-third of the sauce. Repeat the layering in thirds, ending with the cream sauce.

6. Cover the dish with aluminum foil and bake for 25 minutes. Remove the foil and bake for an additional 25 minutes until golden brown and the potatoes are tender. Serve.

Ham And Cheese Palmiers

Servings: 30
Cooking Time: 60 Minutes

Ingredients:

- 1 (9½ by 9-inch) sheet puff pastry, thawed
- 2 tablespoons Dijon mustard
- 2 teaspoons minced fresh thyme
- 2 ounces Parmesan cheese, grated (1 cup)
- 4 ounces thinly sliced deli ham

Directions:

1. Roll puff pastry into 12-inch square on lightly floured counter. Brush evenly with mustard; sprinkle with thyme and Parmesan; pressing gently to adhere, and lay ham evenly over top. Roll up opposite sides of pastry until they meet in middle. Wrap pastry log in plastic wrap and refrigerate until firm, about 1 hour.

2. Adjust toaster oven rack to middle position, select air-fry or convection setting, and preheat the toaster oven to 400 degrees. Line large and small rimmed baking sheets with parchment paper. Using sharp knife, trim ends of log, then slice into ⅓-inch-thick pieces. Space desired number of palmiers at least 1 inch apart on prepared small sheet; space remaining palmiers evenly on prepared large sheet. Re-shape palmiers as needed.

3. Bake small sheet of palmiers until golden brown and crisp, 15 to 25 minutes. Transfer palmiers to wire rack and let cool for 15 minutes before serving. (Palmiers can be held at room temperature for up to 6 hours before serving.)

4. Freeze remaining large sheet of palmiers until firm, about 1 hour. Transfer palmiers to 1-gallon zipper-lock bag and freeze for up to 1 month. Cook frozen palmiers as directed; do not thaw.

Crispy Wontons

Servings: 8
Cooking Time: 10 Minutes

Ingredients:

- ½ cup refried beans
- 3 tablespoons salsa
- ¼ cup canned artichoke hearts, drained and patted dry
- ¼ cup frozen spinach, defrosted and squeezed dry
- 2 ounces cream cheese
- 1½ teaspoons dried oregano, divided
- ¼ teaspoon garlic powder
- ¼ teaspoon onion powder
- ½ teaspoon salt
- ¼ cup chopped pepperoni
- ¼ cup grated mozzarella cheese
- 1 tablespoon grated Parmesan
- 2 ounces cream cheese
- ½ teaspoon dried oregano
- 32 wontons
- 1 cup water

Directions:

1. Preheat the toaster oven to 370°F.

2. In a medium bowl, mix together the refried beans and salsa.

3. In a second medium bowl, mix together the artichoke hearts, spinach, cream cheese, oregano, garlic powder, onion powder, and salt.

4. In a third medium bowl, mix together the pepperoni, mozzarella cheese, Parmesan cheese, cream cheese, and the remaining ½ teaspoon of oregano.

5. Get a towel lightly damp with water and ring it out. While working with the wontons, leave the unfilled wontons under the damp towel so they don't dry out.

6. Working with 8 wontons at a time, place 2 teaspoons of one of the fillings into the center of the wonton, rotating among the different fillings (one filling per wonton). Working one at a time, use a pastry brush, dip the pastry brush into the water, and brush the edges of the dough with the water. Fold the dough in half to form a triangle and set aside. Continue until 8 wontons are formed. Spray the wontons with cooking spray and cover with a dry towel. Repeat until all 32 wontons have been filled.

7. Place the wontons into the air fryer oven, leaving space between the wontons, and air-fry for 5 minutes. Turn over and check for brownness, and then air-fry for another 5 minutes.

Savory Sausage Balls

Servings: 10
Cooking Time: 8 Minutes

Ingredients:

- 2 cups all-purpose flour
- 1 tablespoon baking powder
- ½ teaspoon garlic powder
- ¼ teaspoon onion powder
- ½ teaspoon salt
- 3 tablespoons milk
- 2½ cups grated pepper jack cheese
- 1 pound fresh sausage, casing removed

Directions:

1. Preheat the toaster oven to 370°F.

2. In a large bowl, whisk together the flour, baking powder, garlic powder, onion powder, and salt. Add in the milk, grated cheese, and sausage.

3. Using a tablespoon, scoop out the sausage and roll it between your hands to form a rounded ball. You should end up with approximately 32 balls. Place them in the air fryer oven in a single layer and working in batches as necessary.

4. Air-fry for 8 minutes, or until the outer coating turns light brown.

5. Carefully remove, repeating with the remaining sausage balls.

Smoked Gouda Bacon Macaroni And Cheese

Servings: 10-12

Cooking Time: 30 Minutes

Ingredients:

- 1 (4 oz.) French baguette, torn
- 6 slices cooked bacon, chopped
- 1/4 cup loosely packed parsley
- 2 Tablespoons butter, melted
- 1 package (16 oz.) corkscrew or elbow pasta
- 1/3 cup butter
- 1/4 cup flour
- 4 cups milk
- 1 package (8 oz.) extra sharp Cheddar cheese, shredded
- 1 package (8 oz.) smoked Gouda cheese, shredded
- 2 1/2 teaspoons Creole seasoning

Directions:

1. Preheat the toaster oven to 400°F.

2. Using S-blade with food processor running, drop bread, 1/2 of the bacon and parsley into food chute. Process until finely chopped. Gradually add melted butter; process until crumbs form. Set aside.

3. Cook pasta according to package directions for al dente. Drain and rinse with cold water. Set aside.

4. Melt 1/3 cup butter in Dutch oven over medium-high heat. Gradually add flour, whisking until smooth, about 1 minute. Slowly add milk, stirring 8 to 10 minutes until mixture is thickened and smooth. Remove from heat.

5. Stir in cheeses, remaining bacon and Creole seasoning until cheese is melted. Fold in pasta.

6. Pour mixture into 11x7-inch baking dish sprayed with nonstick cooking spray. Sprinkle with breadcrumb mixture.

7. Bake 25 to 30 minutes or until crumbs are browned and mixture is heated through.

Korean "fried" Chicken Wings

Servings: 4

Cooking Time: 25 Minutes

Ingredients:

- Wings Ingredients
- 2 pounds chicken wings
- 1 teaspoon kosher salt
- ½ teaspoon black pepper
- 1½ teaspoons onion powder
- 1½ teaspoons garlic powder
- ¾ teaspoons ground mustard
- 1 teaspoon gochugaru
- 2 tablespoons cornstarch
- 1 tablespoon water
- Cooking spray
- Toasted sesame seeds, for sprinkling
- Sauce Ingredients
- 3 tablespoons Korean gojuchang red pepper paste
- 2 tablespoon white distilled vinegar
- 1 tablespoon hot water
- 2 tablespoons honey
- 1 tablespoon soy sauce

Directions:

1. Combine all the ingredients for the wings except the cooking spray and sesame seeds in a large bowl. Mix well.

2. Preheat the toaster oven to 400°F.

3. Spray both sides of the wings with cooking spray.

4. Place the wings into the fry basket, then insert the basket at mid position in the preheated oven.

5. Select the Air Fry function, adjust time to 25 minutes, then press Start/Pause.

6. Mix together sauce ingredients until well combined, then microwave on high for 30 seconds. Set aside.

7. Remove wings when done, then place the wings and sauce in a large bowl and toss together until the wings are well coated.

8. Sprinkle the wings with toasted sesame seeds and serve.

Granola Three Ways

Servings: 4
Cooking Time: 10 Minutes

Ingredients:

- Nantucket Granola
- ¼ cup maple syrup
- ¼ cup dark brown sugar
- 1 tablespoon butter
- 1 teaspoon vanilla extract
- 1 cup rolled oats
- ½ cup dried cranberries
- ½ cup walnuts, chopped
- ¼ cup pumpkin seeds
- ¼ cup shredded coconut
- Blueberry Delight
- ¼ cup honey
- ¼ cup light brown sugar
- 1 tablespoon butter
- 1 teaspoon lemon extract
- 1 cup rolled oats
- ½ cup sliced almonds
- ½ cup dried blueberries
- ¼ cup pumpkin seeds
- ¼ cup sunflower seeds
- Cherry Black Forest Mix
- ¼ cup honey
- ¼ cup light brown sugar
- 1 tablespoon butter
- 1 teaspoon almond extract
- 1 cup rolled oats
- ½ cup sliced almonds
- ½ cup dried cherries
- ¼ cup shredded coconut
- ¼ cup dark chocolate chips
- oil for misting or cooking spray

Directions:

1. Combine the syrup or honey, brown sugar, and butter in a small saucepan or microwave-safe bowl. Heat and stir just until butter melts and sugar dissolves. Stir in the extract.

2. Place all other dry ingredients in a large bowl. (For the Cherry Black Forest Mix, don't add the chocolate chips yet.)

3. Pour melted butter mixture over dry ingredients and stir until oat mixture is well coated.

4. Lightly spray a baking pan with oil or cooking spray.

5. Pour granola into pan and air-fry at 390°F for 5 minutes. Stir. Continue cooking for 5 minutes, stirring every minute or two, until golden brown. Watch closely. Once the mixture begins to brown, it will cook quickly.

6. Remove granola from pan and spread on wax paper. It will become crispier as it cools.

7. For the Cherry Black Forest Mix, stir in chocolate chips after granola has cooled completely.

8. Store in an airtight container.

Sausage Cheese Pinwheels

Servings: 16

Cooking Time: 22 Minutes

Ingredients:

- 1 sheet frozen puff pastry, about 9 inches square, thawed (½ of a 17.3-ounce package)
- ½ pound bulk sausage
- ¾ cup shredded cheddar cheese

Directions:

1. Preheat the toaster oven to 400°F. Grease a 12 x 12-inch baking pan.

2. Unfold the puff pastry on a lightly floured surface and roll into a 10 x 12-inch rectangle. Carefully spread the sausage over the surface of the rectangle to within ½ inch of all four edges. Sprinkle the cheese evenly over the sausage. Starting with the long side, roll up tightly and press the edges to seal.

3. Using a serrated knife, slice the roll into ½-inch-thick pieces. You will get about 16 slices. Place the slices, cut side up, in the prepared baking pan. Bake for 18 to 22 minutes or until golden and the sausage is cooked through.

4. Serve warm or at room temperature.

Harissa Roasted Carrots

Servings: 3
Cooking Time: 25 Minutes

Ingredients:

- 1 tablespoon harissa
- 1 tablespoon honey
- 1 tablespoon olive oil
- ¼ teaspoon salt
- 5 large carrots, sliced in half lengthwise
- Chopped parsley, for garnish
- Pomegranate seeds, for garnish
- Chopped toasted walnuts, for garnish

Directions:

1. Combine the harissa, honey, olive oil, and salt in a bowl and whisk together.

2. Select the Preheat function on the Cosori Smart Air Fryer Toaster Oven and press Start/Pause.

3. Line the food tray with foil and place carrots on the tray. Pour the harissa mixture over the carrots and toss to evenly coat.

4. Insert the food tray at mid position in the preheated oven.

5. Select the Bake function, adjust time to 25 minutes, and press Start/Pause.

6. Remove when carrots are golden and tender.

7. Place carrots on a serving platter and garnish with chopped parsley, pomegranate seeds, and walnuts.

RECIPES INDEX

Printed in Great Britain
by Amazon

12697369R10061